GILL'S IRISH LIVES

SEÁN O'CASEY

HUGH HUNT

GILL AND MACMILLAN

First published 1980 by
Gill and Macmillan Ltd
15/17 Eden Quay
Dublin 1
with associated companies in
London, New York, Delhi, Hong Kong,
... Melbourne,

0 7171 1034 6 (paperback)
0 7171 1080 X (hardback)

available in this series:
Michael Collins (Leon O'Broin)
Sean O'Casey (Hugh Hunt)
C. S. Parnell (Paul Bew)
James Craig (Patrick Buckland)
James Joyce (Peter Costello)
Eamon de Valera (T. Ryle Dwyer)

in preparation:
George Bernard Shaw (Kenneth Richards)
W. T. Cosgrave (Maurice Manning)
Daniel O'Connell (Kevin B. Nowlan)
Theobald Wolfe Tone (Henry Boylan)
Edward Carson (A. T. Q. Stewart)
Sean Lemass (Brian Farrell)
Arthur Griffith (Calton Younger)

Origination by Healyset, Dublin
Printed in Great Britain by
Redwood Burn Ltd.
Trowbridge & Esher.

Contents

Prerumble*

All the world's a stage,
And all the men and women merely players;
They have their exits and their entrances,
And one man in his time plays many parts,
His acts being seven ages.
As You Like It, II, vii

Few men can claim to have played so many parts as Seán O'Casey. His 'seven ages' began with Johnny, the half blind Protestant boy, living in a predominantly Catholic community; then came John Casey, the devout church-goer and Sunday-school teacher; Seán Ó Cathasaigh, *alias* 'Irish Jack', the railway labourer and ardent Gaelic enthusiast; then the militant nationalist and member of the Irish Republican Brotherhood. Next came the zealous left-winger, the disciple of Jim Larkin and active organiser of the Irish Citizen Army. The first act closed with a moving death scene in which a son bade farewell to his mother. A brief interval followed during which a few songs were sung, a few poems written. The second act opened with the forty-three-year-old Séan Ó Cathasaigh stepping onto the stage in his star role as Seán O'Casey the playwright. From then on he added some lively sketches and embellishments: Seán the Atheist, Seán the 'blaster and blighter' of religious bigotry, the castigator of capitalism, the courageous champion of sexual freedom, the

*The word 'Prerumble' was coined by O'Casey for the prologue of *The Drums of Father Ned*.

emancipator of youth from middle-class morality.
[2] In these latter roles he appeared in the scarlet robe of a somewhat unorthodox but highly enthusiastic Communist.

Meanwhile behind the scenes was the devoted husband and father, a man of great compassion and courage whose love of Ireland and of his native city, however harsh his criticism of his fellow-countrymen and fellow-Dubliners, was the spring from which his creative work flowed.

He was born in 1880 into a respectable middle-class family whose fortunes declined severely during his early years. Undoubtedly he and his family suffered considerable hardship, but at no time did they live in the overcrowded, disease-ridden Dublin slums as recounted by popular legend and repeated by respectable academics – his early biographers among them.

The first forty-two years of his eventful life were also the most eventful in the history of his country. In the same year as the future dramatist came into the world Charles Stewart Parnell, the 'uncrowned King of Ireland', became leader of the Irish Parliamentary Party in the British House of Commons and there began the long struggle for Home Rule that was to develop into the bloody fight for independence beginning with the Easter Rising in 1916 and ending six years later with the foundation of the Irish Free State. During these years Irish nationalism was growing in strength. The Land League, Arthur Griffith's Sinn Féin and the militant policy adopted by the Irish Republican Brotherhood (IRB) were to lead to the end of seven hundred years of British rule. National identity, too, was strengthened by the Gaelic Athletic Association, dedicated to the cause of Gaelic football and hurling, uncompromising in its hostility to foreign games. More profound and intellectually demanding was the launching of the Gaelic League by Douglas

Hyde in 1893, which made the learning of Irish the hallmark of a true 'Irish Irelander'. These several [3]
gospels were spread throughout the land by a number of political clubs and literary societies, one of which was the St Laurence O'Toole Club with the brave uniforms of its pipers' band and its dramatic activities.

An even more important event in the rebirth of the nation, and in the moulding of its dramatists, was the foundation in 1898 of the Irish Literary Theatre by W. B. Yeats, Lady Gregory and Edward Martyn, in due course to develop into the Irish National Theatre Society with its home in the Abbey Theatre. Thus the stage was set for the birth of a truly national drama, and that moment came in 1903 when John Millington Synge's first play, *In the Shadow of the Glen*, brought the life of the countryside onto the stage, expressed in his unique use of the Anglo-Irish language. Synge's plays and those of Yeats, Lady Gregory, Pádraic Colum, William Boyle and Lennox Robinson set the pattern for Irish drama during the first quarter of the present century.

But the way of life that the early playwrights celebrated was either dying or changing beyond recognition. Another side of Irish life was arising during these years – the growing consciousness of the working-class population of Dublin. It was a life equally rich in language and characters as that portrayed by Synge, and one that was closely related to the momentous events through which the nation was emerging from an almost feudal economy into the 'brave new world' of the 1920s.

In 1908 Jim Larkin arrived in Dublin to preach his 'divine mission of discontent' and to form the Irish Transport and General Workers' Union. This was to lead to a major confrontation between capital and labour and to the great strike and lockout of 1913, from which arose the Irish Citizen Army with its flag

of the plough and the stars. In 1914 came the Great
[4] War, claiming the lives of 60,000 Irishmen and twice that number wounded or maimed for life. There followed the stirring years of Ireland's fight for freedom – the Easter Rising of 1916 and the Anglo-Irish War of 1919–21. Finally came the tragedy of civil strife in 1922–23.

These events were to be the background of the first four plays by O'Casey to be produced on the stage: the Anglo-Irish conflict in *The Shadow of a Gunman*, the Civil War in *Juno and the Paycock*, the 1916 Rising in *The Plough and the Stars*, and the Great War of 1914–18 in *The Silver Tassie.* Later he was to use the lockout of 1913 as part of the background of *Red Roses For Me* and *The Star Turns Red*, though the major influences in these two plays were the 1911 railway strike in the former and the rise of Fascism in the latter.

Yeats was to reprimand him for allowing the background to intrude itself into his plays. 'The whole history of the world must be reduced to wallpaper in front of which the characters must pose and speak,'[1] he wrote in his criticism of *The Silver Tassie*. But to O'Casey the background could never be merely the scenery of his plays. It was a living participant in the drama, a powerful motivating force that moulded his characters as it moulded his life, conditioning his sympathies and his prejudices.

During the forty-one years between the first public presentation of a play by O'Casey in 1923 and his death in 1964 he wrote twenty-five plays (three of which he did not include in his published work), six volumes of autobiography, four volumes of essays, stories and poems, and over one hundred articles, reviews and letters to the press, and kept up a running correspondence with admirers and friends all over the world, his surviving letters alone totalling one and three-quarter million words.[2]

During this highly productive period he chose to exile himself from his native land and from the city in whose streets and among whose people he derived the bright spark that fired his imagination, preferring to live in England against whose domination of Ireland he had in his younger years hurled the barbed spears of his invective. Although an atheist and ardent left-winger, he was nevertheless welcomed in the London drawing-rooms of Lady Londonderry and Lady Astor, and counted among his friends people of such diverse views as Lady Gregory, Jim Larkin, Harold Macmillan, Bernard Shaw, Augustus John, Eugene O'Neill and the influential New York dramatic critics George Jean Nathan and Brooks Atkinson.

In London the critics praised his plays as masterpieces and dismissed them as 'pretentious rubbish'. It was in America that his plays and writings earned him the greater part of his income – though he was never to know financial security. In his own country his books were frequent victims of the rigid censorship laws, and only nine of his plays were produced there during his lifetime. Of these *The Plough and the Stars* produced a first-class riot, and two others, *The Silver Tassie* and *The Bishop's Bonfire*, not only provoked the anger of militant Catholics and nationalists but also incurred the strong criticism of those of a more liberal outlook, some of whom counted themselves among his early admirers and friends.

He himself attacked and counter-attacked, challenging his critics and defending his ideals and seldom missing an opportunity of bringing the full fire-power of his artillery to bear on the kill-joy religious zealots. Yet he, who was so sensitive to criticism, could also criticise unprovoked and sometimes unjustly the work of other writers, among them George Russell (AE), G. K. Chesterton, Noël Coward, W. H. Auden, Denis Johnston, and R. C. Sherriff; and although a lover of

life and youth, a champion of freedom and the cause
[6] of the working classes, he nevertheless found it necessary to defend the ruthless suppression of the workers and students of Hungary in their heroic fight against Soviet tyranny.

'Everything I have written up to the present has been combative,' he wrote to Harold Macmillan, 'and the sword I have swung so long is now stuck in my hand and I can't let go.'[3] His pen was his sword, and from it flowed words in seemingly endless profusion, splendid in their exuberance, fearless in attack, rich indeed in humour. But this flow of words could also overflow the measure of reason and fair comment. 'When I take a pen into my hand something comes over me and I can't help being bitter, even when I write letters,' he told the actress and play director Ria Mooney.[4] Sentiment too could sometimes degenerate into sentimentality, and passion could be demeaned by prejudice. It was this Quixotic compulsion to enter into verbal combat without pausing to consider the consequences or weigh his words that alienated him from so many of his countrymen and denied him the rewards that were due to his genius.

His was essentially a dramatic genius. All that he wrote, not only his plays but even his articles and reviews, bear witness to his theatrical approach. This compulsion to write theatrically was to lead him to break away from the so-called naturalism of the conventional theatre of his time and to venture into new and unfamiliar forms. In doing so he suffered the fate of all who are ahead of their time, and like all courageous adventurers he was to fail as well as succeed.

In the six volumes of his autobiography,[5] O'Casey has bequeathed to the reader a great, if uneven, work of art, but to his biographers a rare confusion of fact and fiction, of misplaced chronology, of characters who have been snatched out of context or whose parts in his life-story have been changed or modified. In the early volumes he followed the example of his countryman [7] James Joyce in presenting real characters under fictitious names. Thus he himself becomes Johnny Casside; his mother, Mrs Casside; his brother Isaac becomes Archie; his sister Isabella, Ella; his first love, Maura Keating, Nora Creena; clergymen, schoolmasters, fellow-workmen and firms for which he worked also appear in disguise. Being essentially a dramatic writer, he could do no other than dramatise his material: selecting, transposing, heightening or frankly inventing to draw forth the laughter and tears for which, as a master of tragi-comedy, he was so rightly acclaimed; using, too, his love of fantasy that was so marked a feature of his later plays.

He would be a bold man who could claim to have written a definitive life of this vital, colourful and gloriously emotional personality. This book makes no such claim. Any contemporary study of O'Casey must, however, benefit from the recent painstaking research into his background and early life. Many of the facts revealed in this book are at variance with the accounts given by his early biographers, who perhaps accepted too readily the fading memories of his ageing contemporaries and, indeed, Seán himself. But truth lies not in facts alone. There remains the greater truth that lies in the heart of the artist. A great heart lies open for all to read in the plays and writing of Seán O'Casey.

1
Johnny Casey

1

The future Sean O'Casey was the last of the five surviving children of Michael and Susan Casey, at least three of whom died in infancy.* Born on 30 March 1880, he was christened John in St Mary's Church in the north and less affluent quarter of the city. Michael Casey was a clerk who had worked for a number of organisations. When Johnny was born he was employed by the Irish Church Missions, whose workers were known by the less complimentary name of 'soupers' – a name derived from their alleged practice of doling out soup to starving peasants during the famine years on condition that they embraced the Protestant faith. Michael Casey was the son of a mixed marriage, his father being a Catholic, his mother a Protestant. Surprisingly, he was brought up as a Protestant. His family were said to be farming folk in Limerick or Kerry. In or before 1863 Michael came to Dublin, where he met and married Susan Archer, an auctioneer's daughter who came from a Wicklow family of staunch Protestants. The family names of Archer, Hall and Harding suggest an Anglo-Irish descent.

In the first volume of his autobiography O'Casey described his father as 'bringing home his two pounds

*In *I Knock at the Door* O'Casey states that he was one of eight children. In *Sunset and Evening Star* the number given is thirteen. Krause and others repeat this number. As the names of only three children who failed to survive appear in the registers, the former figure appears to be correct.

weekly to his wife, like clockwork; liked by many, a little feared by all who knew him, having a gentle, sometimes a fierce habit of criticism; and famed by all as one who spat out his thought into the middle of a body's face'.[1] Called locally 'the scholar', he was clearly a man of some learning. He was familiar with Latin; his library contained books on philosophy, several versions of the Bible, including the Latin Vulgate, a number of polemic works condemning Roman Catholicism, among them *Foxe's Book of Martyrs*, Chillingworth's *Protestantism* and Merle d'Aubigny's *History of the Reformation*, from which the future castigator of Irish Catholicism came to know 'a lot about . . . sturdy Luther, fiery Zwingli, scholarly Erasmus. God's own job they had to overthrow the idea of the Pope's supremacy in the hearts of the people; and harder still to turn the Church that had become the church of Babylon back into the church of God.'[2] Equally influential in the formative years of the future playwright were standard English classics, especially the novels of Dickens and the poetry of Byron, Burns, Keats and Shelley; all of these appeared on the well-stocked shelves of his father's library; and, of course, there were the plays of Shakespeare.

That Michael Casey was also a man of some substance is evident from the appearance of his name in the list of 'nobility, gentry, merchants and traders of the city of Dublin'. While this does not put him into the so-called 'garrison' class, it does put an end, once and for all, to the legend of the slums.

Johnny Casey was a sickly child. At six months old he developed acute bronchitis. At the age of five his left eye developed an ulcerated cornea, causing him intense pain when exposed to any form of bright light. This involved frequent visits to the eye clinic, as a result of which his schooling was affected; though the belief that he had no formal education is as legendary

as the story of his slum origin. His eye affliction con-
[10] tinued throughout his life, culminating in almost total blindness during his latter years.

Michael Casey held firmly to the Protestant ideals of hard work combined with a sound education. For this reason he did not send the three older children to the National Schools, where free education was available, but to the fee-paying Central Model Schools in Marlborough Street, where George Bernard Shaw was educated. Isabella Charlotte (Bella), the eldest of the Casey children – she was born in 1865 – seems to have been the most industrious. She graduated with honours in four subjects, including French, and was also an accomplished pianist. After two years in Marlborough Street Teacher Training College she was appointed as a principal teacher at St Mary's Infants' School, attached to the local National School. Michael Harding (Mick), the second eldest, showed some talent as an artist. His father wanted him to become an architect, but both he and his brother Thomas Hall (Tom) were idle scholars who had to receive private tutoring to get them through their exams. They too obtained teaching certificates but preferred to seek employment in the Post Office service. Isaac Archer (known as Archie in the life-story), who was seven years older than Johnny, was denied the benefits of post-school education by reason of his father's death and the consequent change in the family fortunes. This occurred in September 1886. In January of that year Michael Casey was forced to leave his job owing to a spinal injury that left him partially paralysed. He was granted a gratuity amounting to three months' salary in recognition of his loyal service, but this was quickly swallowed up in medical costs and by funeral arrangements of a remarkably lavish kind. In his life-story O'Casey records a closed hearse, three carriages, twenty-six cabs and six side-cars. As the estate was not admitted to probate, presumably there was little left for his family.

When Johnny came into the world the family was living at 85 Upper Dorset Street in the parish of St Mary's, a comparatively large house that has since been replaced by a bank. Research confirms it to have been of three or four storeys and containing at least seven or eight rooms. It was owned by a local landlord, William Lattimer. Michael Casey was the sole listed tenant and ratepayer. O'Casey told his biographer, David Krause, that his father was the caretaker, letting out rooms on behalf of the landlord. When Bella left to become a student at her training college, and subsequently a living-in teacher at the infants' school, the family moved to 9 Inisfallen Parade, a much smaller house in the same parish. It was here that Michael Casey died at the early age of forty-nine.

2

While it would seem that the future Seán O'Casey inherited much of his father's temperament, it was his mother who was the major influence in his early life. As the last of her children, and a sickly one as well, he inevitably claimed the greater part of her affection after her husband's death. Probably she spoilt him. At all events his dependence on her bred in him a possessiveness resulting in tensions between him and his brothers. This, combined with his eye affliction and the gap in years between his brothers and himself, meant that during these early formative years young Johnny was a comparatively isolated figure in the Casey family, living an imaginative life of his own and developing a remarkable ability to learn by heart passages from books read to him by his mother and sister.

His schooling began in 1885, a year before his

father's death. Probably it was due to his eye disease that he was sent to St Mary's Infants' School, where Bella could look after him, instead of following his brothers to a fee-paying institution. During his first two years he was often absent from class, but thereafter he was in fairly constant attendance. He was clearly a bright pupil, passing all three of his annual examinations in reading, two of them with honours. After moving up to first grade he was equally successful in spelling and maths. At his Sunday-school he received an illuminated scroll for 'proficiency in Holy Scripture and Church Formularies'.

Many years later O'Casey informed Lady Gregory that he did not learn to read until he was sixteen.[3] He subsequently explained his success in his exams by learning the required passages by heart, thus leading his examiners to believe that he was reading them.[4] On the other hand, Gabriel Fallon was told by O'Casey that his mother taught him to read at an early age.[5] Perhaps there is truth in all these statements: sight-reading would have been a major problem for the half-blind child, and there is evidence that young Johnny possessed remarkable ability to memorise passages that were only read to him once.

In 1887 the family income was further reduced when Tom and Mick left their secure and comparatively well-paid jobs to enlist in the army. Presumably they were influenced in making this decision through their friendship with Nicholas Beaver (Bugler Benson in the life-story), a professional soldier who was courting Bella at the time (they were married in 1889). Both her sons' departure and her daughter's marriage were a blow to Susan Casey's pride. A common soldier was distinctly a drop in Protestant social values. Despite the fact that Beaver was a Protestant, Susan showed her disapproval by refusing to attend the wedding. She was to do the same later when Tom and Isaac married Catholic girls.

Susan Casey was described by those who knew her as 'a neat little woman who wore a pretty bonnet and distributed sweets'.[6] A studio photograph of her holding her infant granddaughter shows her as a well-dressed woman, a far cry from the typical 'shawlie' of Dublin's slums. O'Casey has drawn his own portrait of this valiant woman in his autobiographies as Mrs Casside, and in his play *Red Roses For Me* as Mrs Breydon, as one who, undaunted by the blows of ill-fortune and holding her head high among her neighbours, was yet ever willing to lend a hand to those in distress, while struggling herself with increasing poverty to feed her family and maintain its respectability. To be a Protestant and poor in Ireland was tantamount to an admission of failure at a time when the ruling class was the prosperous Protestant minority and the Catholics were regarded as the feckless poor.

Christopher Casey, a nephew of the playwright, stated that his uncle 'was not a poor boy as depicted by some of the writers. While he was with the O'Caseys he never knew what want was.'[7] His first love, Maura Keating, declared that 'Seán always wanted people to think he was a lot worse off than he really was in his early days. He liked to put on the Irish man's poor mouth.'[8]

Poverty is relative to the status of the family or individual. There is no doubt that the decline in the family's fortunes after the death of the father and the loss of income occasioned by the departure of the two eldest boys brought hardship. There was worse to come. Bella's marriage entailed her relinquishing her job as a schoolteacher. Her husband was serving in England, and she was forced to seek shelter with her mother. Fortunately in 1888 Isaac found employment as an office-boy for the *Daily Express*. His weekly wage of 15s was for a time the main source of the family finances.

Economic pressures once again forced the family [14] to move, this time to a neighbourhood in the north-east corner of the city. Their new home, 25 Hawthorn Terrace, was and still is one of a row of single-storey houses, each consisting of two rooms and a kitchen. In the back yard was a water-tap and a dry privy, the contents of which were, as O'Casey was later to relate, carried through the house in baskets by the sanitation men.[9] By today's standards this again would seem to indicate that the family had sunk to the bottom of the social scale, but at the time the street was populated by lower middle-class people of modest means. The new home lay in the Church of Ireland parish of St Barnabas, later to appear in *Red Roses For Me* and in the life-story as St Burnupus. Like St Mary's, the parish supported its own National School. It was probably in this school rather than in St Mary's that the incident occurred that brought an end to Johnny's formal education.[10] O'Casey related how, after he had been unjustly caned by his sadistic form-master and made to stand on a chair behind the master's desk – surely an unwise decision – he picked up an ebony ruler and cracked it on the head of his tormentor. Upon which the rector of the parish called upon Mrs Casey, demanding that her son be severely caned before the whole school and made to go down on his knees to beg forgiveness. Susan Casey indignantly refused, and Johnny was withdrawn from the school.

He was now nine years old. The pain in his eyes was temporarily relieved by the treatment prescribed at the eye clinic, St Mark's Ophthalmic Hospital for Accidents and Diseases of the Eye and Ear.

> Now he could jump into the sunlight, laugh, sing, shout, dance and make merry in his heart, with no eye to see what he was doing save only the eye of God, far away behind the blue sky in the daytime,

and farther away still behind the golden stare of the night-time.[11]

His father, before he died, had voiced the fear that, as a result of Johnny's weak eyesight, he might grow up a dunce. This would mean little chance of his obtaining respectable and lucrative employment as befitted a member of the Protestant community. The problem of furthering his education was the urgent concern of his mother. The Bluecoat School was suggested, but Susan Casey was unwilling to have her favourite child brought up in an institution. The greater part of his future education was therefore undertaken by his sister, using books left over from the sale of their father's library. Johnny was a stubborn child. Fetching him in from playing in the street to learn his lessons involved a struggle of wills.

– I'm not goin' to do it, he said viciously: I won't do it. I'm good enough as I am.

– Very well, said his mother firmly, at the end of the week, no penny for your *Boys of London and New York*. Remember, no lessons, no penny for your paper.

Johnny was beaten. He'd as lief lose his life as lose the stories of *Old King Brady*, *The Wonder Detective*, *Red Eagle*, *The Friend of the Palefaces*, or *From Bootblack to Broker*, the story of business life in New York, all of which his mother helped him to read when he brought the paper home.[12]

Religious duties played an important part in his education. Regular attendance at church and Sunday-school was strictly maintained; grace was said before meals, and Susan Casey read him passages from the Bible that he learned by heart; all contributing to his growing delight in language. More than anything else was the revelation of a new world that opened up for him in the plays of Shakespeare and Boucicault.

3

[16] During the last decade of the nineteenth century and the early years of the twentieth, amateur drama was all the rage. Dublin bristled with dramatic societies, partly inspired by the greater frequency of visiting theatre companies from overseas, now made possible by improvements in rail and steamship services, partly by the growth and popularity of melodrama, notably the plays of Dion Boucicault and the patriotic dramas presented at the Queen's Theatre.

Isaac Casey was among the many keen amateur actors of the time. A stage was constructed in the living-room of Hawthorn Terrace where extracts from *Dick's Standard Plays*, most notably those of Shakespeare and Boucicault, were given with the help of recruits drawn from the children of the neighbourhood and including the family mongrel. Among Isaac's friends was Charles Dalton (Tommie Talton in the life-story),[13] an actor-manager in one of the barnstorming touring companies of the time. With his help a disused stable in Hill Street was converted into a theatre. The partitions were scrapped, a stage erected at one end, and

> Ould lanterns, bought second-hand, shaded with cardboard, coloured yellow and black, did well as footlights; and a turkey-red twill curtain went up or came down at the ringing of a handbell. The stage was fitted with lovely parlour, hall, and landscape sets, provided with better parts of old canvas cut away from old cloth thrown away by the Queen's Theatre. Here sketches were given to audiences of forty or fifty, who paid twopence a head to get in, to see Archie [Isaac] playing the Duke of Gloucester, to Johnny's Henry the Sixth.[14]

Many years later O'Casey was to open his play, *Red Roses For Me* with a scene in which the young railway worker, Ayamonn Breydon, modelled on a romanticised self-portrait, is seen rehearsing the same play. This time, however, it is he who is to play the more rewarding part of the Duke of Gloucester.

Equally popular were the plays of Dion Boucicault, admired by Synge and Shaw as well as O'Casey. From his plays the future playwright was to discover that juxtaposition of farce and tragedy which became one of the major characteristics of the O'Casey style. It was as a result of young Johnny's playing of Father Dolan in Boucicault's ever-popular melodrama, *The Shaughraun*, that the fifteen-year-old Johnny Casey was chosen by Dalton to stand in for an actor who had fallen sick when his company were performing this play at the old Mechanics' Theatre in Abbey Street. Thus it came about that he appeared on the stage of the theatre that nine years later was to be transformed into the Abbey Theatre in which he was to win his first laurels as a playwright.

His growing fascination with the theatre was further stimulated by visits to the Queen's Theatre. Through a brother-in-law of the Dalton family he obtained a free pass to see the great melodrama of the time, *The Corsican Brothers*, *Saved From the Sea* and the plays of Boucicault.[15] But it was Shakespeare above all that was his favourite. 'Shakespeare was my education,' he told George Bishop of the London *Observer* many years later. 'When I was a boy in Dublin thirty years ago, the Benson Company came to the city, and I spent all my small wages and went without food in order to see all the plays that were performed.'[16]

4

During the 1890s the Casey family's fortunes rose and fell. Mick was discharged from the army as unfit in 1893, and Tom completed his term of service in

1895; both regained their jobs in the Post Office,
[18] bringing a welcome addition to the family budget. Nicholas Beaver also completed his service around this time, obtaining employment with the Great Northern Railway Company, so that he and Bella were able to establish their own household with a growing number of children. Isaac's wages were increasing, and in 1894 Johnny reached the age of fourteen, when boys normally left school. He signed on as a dispatch clerk and stock-boy with Hampton-Leedom & Co. (Hymdim, Leadem & Co. in the life-story), 'wholesale chandlers of Henry Street, dealing in china, delph and hardware'. From his weekly wage of 6s he gave 4s 6d to his mother, and the rest went on books. 'The first serious book I ever bought was a shilling copy of the Globe edition of Shakespeare, and I learnt Hamlet, Macbeth and Julius Caesar by heart' he was to declare to an interviewer in London in 1926.[17] Sometimes, as he tells us, his library was increased by less honest means. In his life-story he admits not only to filching the occasional book but to nefarious activities on a wider scale, rather surprisingly informing us that the upright and God-fearing Susan Casey, far from condemning such practices, sewed larger pockets in his coat to facilitate his illegal operations! Tom also was able to bring some welcome gifts to the household by encouraging the odd crate to fall from the van and spill its contents in his direction.

In 1896 or 1897 young John Casey's first job came to an abrupt end. For some time past he had been incurring the displeasure of the principals of the firm by his cheeky attitude. Finally he was sacked for protesting at being fined two shillings for impertinence. It may have been due to a drop in the family's finances that led Susan Casey to move house once again, for Tom was out of work for some time with a severe illness and Isaac had decided to try his luck on the stage by joining one of the theatrical companies touring the country towns.

The new home, 18 Abercorn Road, was a two-roomed apartment in a somewhat dingy two-storey house in the immediate vicinity of St Barnabas's Church, the rest of the house being occupied by a Catholic family. Three or four boys occupying one room may seem today like slum conditions, and there were, as related in the life-story, bugs to contend with. At the time, however, it was very far from the over-crowding of the Dublin slum tenements, and the neighbourhood itself was quiet and respectable. But there is no doubt that the Caseys, by becoming tenants instead of householders, had come down in the social scale. Part, at least, of the bitterness that O'Casey was to display against the capitalist system must have been born from these years of his family's continuous descent from the comparative comfort and security of his early childhood to what was now and in the future to be a condition of humiliating poverty. So far, however, the young rebel had not fully emerged, and like his mother, he remained a loyal Unionist and devout Christian.

In the young curate of St Barnabas, the Rev. Harry Fletcher, a graduate of Trinity College, John found a good friend and mentor. In 1898 Fletcher prepared the eighteen-year-old youth for confirmation, and when John lost his job with Hampton-Leedom, he obtained employment for him with the stationers and wholesale newsagents Eason & Son (Jason & Sons in the life-story). Here he was even less successful than in his first job. He was dismissed after a week for refusing to take off his cap while receiving his pay. Fletcher was a high churchman, known at the time as a 'ritualist'. The high church ritual that he introduced in his services aroused the anger of those members of the select vestry who belonged to the Orange Order.

Windows were smashed, the organist knocked uncon-
[20] scious, and demands were made for Fletcher's resig-
nation. Young John Casey fought hard to win him popular support, but his efforts were in vain and Fletcher was forced to leave.

By 1898 Isaac had abandoned his brief stage career and found more secure employment as a clerk in Messrs Harmsworth's publishing agency, where he was able to get John a temporary job at 5s a week. This too seems to have been of brief duration. Later John was to find employment as a navvy for the Great Northern Railway, working on the line from Dublin to Malahide. From all this it would seem that John, or 'Irish Jack' as he came to be known, was not cut out for a servile life. His nephew, Christopher Casey, who admitted to no particular love for his 'Uncle Jack', described him as 'a square peg in a round hole'.[18]

Meanwhile his true interests were developing as he applied himself passionately to reading everything he could lay his hands on: the novels of Dickens, Scott, Balzac and Victor Hugo, the poetry of the romantics, history both classical and modern, Darwin's *Origin of Species* and *Descent of Man*, Bunyan's *Pilgrim's Progress*, together with the remaining religious books of his father, 'all backed up with Chambers' Dictionary'.

In 1899 the Boer War broke out, and Tom, as a reservist, was recalled to the colours. John accompanied him to the boat, carrying his rifle. Tom's service in South Africa must have been short, for he was discharged in November 1900. During his absence the sole contributors to the household were presumably Mick and Isaac. The latter's contribution probably ceased in April of the following year when, much against Susan Casey's wishes, he married a Catholic girl and left home. In the same year the Rev. Edward Griffin became Rector of St Barnabas.

He too had to face opposition from the Orange members of the congregation. Once again John took up [21] the cudgels on the new rector's behalf – this time successfully. The dissidents were routed at an election to the select vestry. Edward Griffin proved to be a close friend and father-figure to the young John Casey. The third volume of his autobiographies, *Drums Under the Window*, carried the photograph of this gentle and austere priest with the inscription: 'The Rev. E. M. Griffin, B.D., M.A., who, by refusing to be either Orangeman or Freemason, kept the door of the church open for all to enter'. O'Casey was to portray him in *Red Roses For Me* as the Rev. E. Clinton, the sympathetic Rector of St Burnupus.

From 1900 to 1903 John Casey taught in the St Barnabas Sunday-school. At the same time he was also a regular attender at the rector's weekly prayer-meetings. One of Mr Griffin's daughters has provided a description of John when, at the conclusion of the service, the rector used to ask for a volunteer to lead the final prayer:

> It was then after an awkward pause, while Father waited for the volunteer, that my sister and I – we were girls of eight and ten – would nudge each other and whisper, "It'll be John again" – He was John to us, not Seán – "he'll jump up again, and oh, he'll go on and on as he always does." He sat behind us and we were afraid to turn round and look, but soon we heard his voice ringing out loud and clear, in that drawling, lilting way he had of speaking. He didn't read from the prayer-book as the others did, he just made up his prayers as he went along, using some biblical phrases but mostly his own words about the glory of God. As I said, at the time my sister and I joked about how he would go on and on with it, but we were silly little

girls then, and when I think of it all now it comes
[22] back to me as something very moving and beautiful. He would have made a great preacher.[19]

2
Seán Ó Cathasaigh

1

John Casey was twenty-three when he took up pick and shovel to work for the Great Northern Railway. With neither instrument was he particularly successful – at least not at first.

> His arms had grown into things torturing his body, and his gasping breath seemed to cling to where it was in his lungs, stifling him, rather than to tear a way through his gasping mouth. Sweat was hiding the blue sky above him; the sky itself was damp with sweat, the whole earth was tired and aching, all save only those dim figures working at his side, laughing silently at him for thinking he could become a navvy; but it was for food, for security, for freedom from want, and stick it he must.[1]

No doubt it was to restore his self-esteem that he began to search for other areas where he might gain greater recognition and more congenial company. These were the days when to gaelicise your name and to learn Irish were the hallmarks of the educated young patriots of the middle classes. In 1902 or 1903 John joined the Drumcondra branch of the Gaelic League, gaelicising his name to Seán Ó Cathasaigh and learning the language with the aid of Father O'Growney's *Simple Lessons in Irish*.

In the early 1900s members of the Gaelic League were increasingly turning to more extreme forms of nationalism. Seán joined the Gaelic Athletic Associa-

tion some time before 1905; from there it was but
[24] a short step to membership of the Irish Republican Brotherhood and to a complete break with the Unionist views of his family. To keep the peace at home Susan Casey had to ban the discussion of politics at table. At the same time he continued to be actively involved with the affairs of the Church. He was concerned with the introduction of Irish-speaking clergy as preachers in Dublin churches and with persuading Protestants to join the national movement. Among those who responded to his urgings was the young Ernest Blythe, later to become a member of the first Free State government and eventually managing director of the Abbey Theatre. Blythe was inducted by Seán into the IRB, probably in 1905. In *Trasna na Bóinne* (Across the Boyne)[2] Blythe relates how he first met the future playwright at a hurling match, a sport for which Seán's weak eyesight made him something of a hazard to his fellow-players. On one occasion, it is said, he killed a sparrow in the belief that he was swiping at the ball![3]

Already Seán was beginning to write. His first article to be published, 'Sound the Loud Trumpet', a bitter attack on the government's education policy concluding with a denunciation of British rule in Ireland, was published in W. P. Ryan's paper, the *Irish Peasant*, on 25 May 1907. In 1906 he had become secretary of the Drumcondra branch of the Gaelic League, earning a reputation as a powerful and persuasive speaker and inducing, according to Blythe, ninety per cent of the membership to join the IRB.

In 1907 Seán joined the St Laurence O'Toole Club. Nominally a social club, its members were, however, largely nationalist in outlook. Seán became a close friend of a fellow-member, Frank Cahill, an ardent republican and nationalist. Together they formed the St Laurence O'Toole Pipers' Band. Seán himself, however, was no piper. His attempts to practise the bagpipes, whether at home or elsewhere, were effectively terminated by his brother Mick puncturing the instrument with an awl. As secretary of the band Seán successfully organised performances and acted as publicity agent. Less successful were his attempts to persuade his fellow railway workers to join the Gaelic League.

> What would the nicely-suited, white-collared respectable members of the refined Gaelic League branches of Dublin do if they found themselves in the company of these men? Toiling, drinking, whoring, they lived everywhere and anywhere they could find a ready-made lodging or room. They didn't remember the glories of Brian the Brave. Beyond knowing him as an oul' king of Ireland in God's time, they knew nothing and cared less. Their upper life was a hurried farewell to the *News of the World* on Sunday morning, and a dash to what was called short twelve Mass in the Pro-Cathedral, the shortest Mass said in the land; and then a slow parade to the various pubs, and a wearisome wait till the pubs unveiled themselves by sliding the shutters down, and let the mass of men crowd in for refreshment. And yet Seán felt in his heart that these men were all-important in anything to be done for Ireland.[4]

Meanwhile his religious fervour was fast dying down, though his attachment to Edward Griffin and his delight in the language of the Bible and the Book of Common Prayer never wavered. But Darwin's *Descent of Man* and the new 'higher criticism' had shaken the foundations of 'fundamentalism', and to Seán the Bible no longer appeared to have been handed down from heaven by God's right hand 'or His left one either . . . all made up with chapter and verse and

bound in a golden calfskin'.[5] The death of his favourite
[26] brother, Tom, at the age of forty-four in 1914; the tribulations of his sister – her husband insane and she and her children destitute and homeless; his contact with the wretched living conditions, the hunger and disease of the slums in which Bella was now forced to live; all contributed to his loss of faith. Then, too, his growing nationalism, impregnated with the republican principles of the IRB, was generally inimical to the loyalist views of the Church of Ireland, and even more so to the Catholic hierarchy, for whom the republicanism inherited from Wolfe Tone smelt of the horrors of the French Revolution. Even the enthusiastic movement for the revival of the Irish language incurred the disapproval of the Catholic bishops when it threatened to interfere with their role as spokesmen on matters affecting Catholic education. This was amply demonstrated by the O'Hickey case of 1909.

In that year the Rev. Dr Michael O'Hickey, Professor of Irish at St Patrick's College, Maynooth, the national Catholic seminary, published a pamphlet advocating Irish as a compulsory matriculation requirement at the newly established National University. However, the Standing Committee of the Irish hierarchy had already issued an official pronouncement making plain their own opposition, on strategic grounds, to the introduction of compulsory Irish. O'Hickey's action was seen as an insubordinate and potentially disruptive intervention, and when he continued to issue public attacks on the hierarchy for their pusillanimity on the language question, he was ordered to desist and to retract his statements. He refused to be muzzled and was thereupon summarily dismissed from his post by the college senate, acting under strong pressure from the autocratic Cardinal Logue.

Here was a cause that immediately aroused the

fighting spirit of Seán the nationalist and Irish-Irelander. For the first time we see Seán in his life-long role of crusader against ecclesiastical tyranny, calling on republicans, nationalists and Gaelic Leaguers to rise up and demand the reinstatement of O'Hickey, but his efforts were in vain for neither Sinn Féiners nor Leaguers could afford to incur the hostility of the bishops. So Dr O'Hickey was abandoned to fight a lonely and frustrating battle in Rome and to be finally defeated by the pressures and promptings of the Irish caucus and of Cardinal Logue himself. In 1916 he died in Ireland, impoverished and forgotten. But by Seán he was to be commemorated as a martyred hero in a chapter of *Drums Under the Window*, together with his friend Dr Walter McDonald, Professor of Theology, six of whose books were suppressed by the Church and who, alone among the senior academics of Maynooth, supported him. To each of these rebels against ecclesiastical authority Seán was to dedicate a volume of his autobiographies. Strange as it may seem that he, who had renounced his faith and was a bitter critic of the Church, should dedicate his work to two churchmen, yet Seán was ever a champion of those who fought against what he considered to be a denial of life and freedom, be they priest or layman.

Soon he was to find a new cause to champion, and with it a new hero. In 1911, as the relations between capital and labour in Dublin were deteriorating towards a headlong clash, he joined Jim Larkin's Irish Transport and General Workers' Union.

2

In December 1911 Seán was dismissed from his job with the railway company, ostensibly on grounds of unsatisfactory work. Actually his dismissal was motivated by his criticisms of the working conditions and his refusal to sign a document undertaking not

to join Larkin's union. In Jim Larkin, Seán found a
[28] prophet of a new religion, crying

> not for an assignation with peace, dark obedience, or placid resignation; but trumpet-tongued of resistance to wrong, discontent with leering poverty and defiance of any power strutting out to stand in the way of their march forward . . . . Here was the word En-Masse, not handed down from Heaven, but handed up from a man.[6]

Unemployment brought real hardship to Seán and his mother, with nothing but her small pension to keep them both. During the months he was out of work it was little more than 'dry bread and tea, with an odd herring when they happened to be tuppence a dozen'. For weeks on end he was confined to bed with a form of paralysis of the legs, nursed by his mother, who was too proud to let him go to the infirmary. Eventually temporary employment was found for him as a builder's labourer.

Joxer: What are you wearin' your moleskin trousers for?

Boyle: I have to go to a job, Joxer. Just after you'd gone, Devine kem runnin' in to tell us that Father Farrell said if I went down to the job that's goin' on in Rathmines I'd get a start.

Joxer: Be the holy, that's good news!

Boyle: How is it good news? I wonder if you were in my condition, would you call it good news?

Joxer: I thought . . .

Boyle: You thought! You think too sudden sometimes, Joxer. D'ye know, I'm hardly able to crawl with the pain in me legs!

Joxer: Yis, yis; I forgot the pain in your legs. I know you can do nothin' while they're at you.

Boyle: You forgot; I don't think any of yous realise the state I'm in with the pain in my legs. What ud happen if I had to carry a bag of cement?

Joxer: Ah, any man havin' the like of them pains ud be down an' out, down an' out.

(*Juno and the Paycock*, Act 1)

As a builder's labourer Seán could only gain spasmodic employment. However, his time was not wasted, for now he was free to read Emerson, Zola, Whitman and Shaw, for whom he developed a lifelong admiration. He was free, too, to devote himself to the cause of Jim Larkin, his 'Prometheus Hibernica'. From June 1912 onwards he was writing letters and articles for Larkin's paper, the *Irish Worker*, and for the nationalist periodical *Irish Freedom*. But his nationalist views were undergoing a change. The revival of the language and the overthrow of British rule must, he now believed, be allied to the political philosophy of the Labour movement. The cause must no longer be an Irish Republic, but an Irish Workers' Republic. At first he hoped by persuasion to graft the Labour cause onto the nationalist movement, but this was liked by neither the Gaelic League nor the Irish Republican Brotherhood, nor was he himself popular in either camp. Already he had narrowly escaped being turned out of the Drumcondra Branch of the League for declaring his admiration of Synge's *Playboy of the Western World*, condemned by both nationalists and the Church, though it is unlikely that he had seen the play. He was equally out of favour with the IRB for his criticisms of what he had held to be the weakness of their policy, while the Brotherhood itself had no wish to introduce sectional interests which would inevitably lead to a split in its ranks. When he failed to get Larkin's Labour cause accepted he resigned from both the Gaelic League and the IRB and became increasingly hostile to what he considered middle-class nationalism. However, he remained a member of the St Laurence O'Toole Club

and in July 1913 became secretary of the Wolfe Tone
[30] Memorial Committee, responsible for organising the annual pilgrimage to the grave of the 1798 hero in Bodenstown.

> *Peter:* Are you goin' to start th' young Covey's game o' proddin' and twartin' a man? There's not many that's talkin' can say that for twenty-five years he never missed a pilgrimage to Bodenstown!
>
> *Fluther:* You're always blowin' about goin' to Bodenstown. D'ye think no one but yourself ever went to Bodenstown?
>
> *Peter (plaintively):* I'm not blowin' about it; but there's not a year that I go there but I pluck a leaf off Tone's grave, and this very year me prayer-book is nearly full of them.
>
> *Fluther (scornfully):* Then Fluther has a vice versa opinion of them that put ivy leaves in their prayer-books, scabbin' it on the clergy, an' thryin' to out-do th' haloes o' th' saints be lookin' as if he was wearin' around his head a glittherin' aroree boree allis.
>
> (*The Plough and the Stars*, Act 3)

In August 1913 came the lockout that not only deprived him of earning a livelihood, but also led him yet further along the path at the end of which he was to exchange the green banner for the red.

By 1913 Larkin's challenge to the bosses of Irish industry had won considerable success. Although a serious railway strike in 1911 and a number of local stoppages had not in fact done much to improve wages, Larkin's stirring speeches were making the workers increasingly aware of their potential power. Membership of the ITGWU rose from 4,000 in 1911 to some 10,000 by the middle of 1913. To William Martin Murphy, one of Dublin's most powerful tycoons, it was clear that Larkin and the growing Labour movement would have to be challenged. In August 1913 Larkin turned his attention to one of Murphy's many enterprises, the Dublin United Tramways Company, pressing for an extra shilling a week for all workers. Murphy opened his attack by refusing to recognise Larkin or his union. In reply Larkin called the tramway men out on strike during Horse Show week, the high point of the social season. Murphy now managed to persuade the hitherto hesitant Employers' Federation to close ranks and counterattack by locking out all members of Larkin's union, whereupon Larkin called for a general strike. By the end of September 25,000 men and their families were facing a grim winter of cold and starvation. Tempers rose to fever pitch when two people were killed and many hundreds wounded in a police baton-charge during a demonstation addressed by Larkin. Among the crowd on that day was Seán O'Casey.

'Seán shivered, for he was not a hero, and he felt it was unwise to have come here. He felt in his pocket: yes, the strip of rag and his one handkerchief were safe there. It was well to have something to use for a bandage, for a body never knew where or how a sudden wound would rise.'[7] Thirty-nine years later in *Red Roses For Me* an idealised Seán in the person of Ayamonn Breydon was among those who fell a victim to the charge of the police.

As a defence against further attacks on the workers, Larkin and others formed the Irish Citizen Army in the autumn of 1913. Shortly afterwards another paramilitary organisation, the Irish National Volunteers, was formed. This body, largely officered by middle-class nationalists and better organised and equipped than the ICA, drew many recruits away from the Citizen Army and split the separatist movement into two potentially hostile factions. Seán was now fully

active in Liberty Hall, the headquarters of the ITGWU.
[32] Through the medium of the *Irish Worker* he attacked the leadership of the Volunteers. At the same time he tried to persuade the deserters from the Citizen Army to return to the Labour camp.

> Many of you have been tempted to join this much talked of movement by the wild impulse of genuine enthusiasm. You have again allowed yourselves to be led away by words – words – words! You have again forgotten that there can be no interests outside those identified with your class. That every worker must separate himself from every party – every movement that does not tend towards the development of the faith that all power springs from and is invested in the people.[8]

He was now acting as secretary of the Strikers' Relief Committee, raising funds for clothing for their wives and children and contributing to the entertainments and social evenings to keep the men and their families from brooding over their sufferings. But by January 1914 cold and hunger had won the day and resistance to the lockout was declining. In order to prevent the complete disintegration of the Labour movement, Seán suggested the reorganisation of the Citizen Army on a permanent basis. At a general meeting in March he was elected as honorary secretary of a new Army Council. Equipment and uniforms were ordered, camps and manoeuvres were organised, and regular drilling took place. But recruitment was slow and was almost entirely confined to the city, while hostility persisted between the ICA and the Volunteers.

With the outbreak of the Great War the Volunteers split in two, the great majority following the parliamentary leader, John Redmond, pledged to aid the cause of Great Britain and the Empire, while a militant nationalist minority, now heavily infiltrated by the IRB secretly prepared for revolt against Britain. Reconciliation of the Citizen Army with this militant wing was strongly urged by Countess Markievicz, who was a member of both organisations. Seán, who had little liking for the so-called 'Red Countess', now moved a resolution demanding that she sever her connection either with the Irish Volunteers or the Irish Citizen Army. His resolution was defeated and he was called upon to apologise. He refused and promptly resigned.

3

Seán's participation in the formation of the Irish Citizen Army and in the 1913 lockout made it impossible for him to get a job. Unemployment led to undernourishment, and this was probably partly the cause of a further ailment. In August 1915 tubercular glands began to swell in his neck: 'I had a lump there as big as an apple.'[9] Through the ITGWU he obtained a bed in St Vincent's Hospital for the necessary operation. He was lucky, for Dublin's hospitals were overcrowded with many hundreds of wounded soldiers newly arrived from France. During his spell in hospital new thoughts were born in his head as he listened to accounts of 'the slime, the blooded mud, the crater, and the shell-hole had become God's kingdom on earth'.[10] The disturbing visions that now filled his mind were to be recaptured many years later when a war-wounded soldier, once a great footballer but now crippled for life, cried out in despair in just such a hospital: 'God of the miracles, give a poor devil a chance, give a poor devil a chance!' and off-stage the nuns are heard singing in the convent chapel:

> Salve Regina, mater misericordiae;
> Vitae dulcedo et spes nostra salve!

Slowly but surely the playwright was being born.

[34] Despite the care and kindness of the nuns, Seán was to fall foul of them as he had done, and was to do, with so many of his friends and fellow-workers. Stung by some disparaging remarks about Larkin made by one of the ward sisters, he 'wrapped his razor, soap, brush and face flannel in an old ragged handkerchief' and walked out.[11]

In October 1915 Larkin left Ireland to raise funds for the ITGWU in America. Seán's attachment to the Labour movement now began to wane. This was partly due to the fact that he no longer enjoyed the same relationship with the leadership as he had done with Larkin, but also to an antipathy to Larkin's successor, James Connolly, and to his policy of gradually edging the movement towards a nationalist, as opposed to a predominantly socialist, outlook. Seán feared that this would lead to the eventual submergence of the cause of Labour. His fears were justified. The rapprochement between Connolly and Pearse in January 1916 that preceded the abortive Easter Rising, in which both men were to sacrifice their lives, resulted in the almost total disappearance of the Labour movement in Ireland for many years to come.

Seán took no part in the Rising. There is little doubt he had become an embarrassment to Connolly and the new leadership. Moreover, he had discovered that he was not cut out to be a hero. To write brave words advocating striking 'a blow for Ireland' was very different from 'the humming zipzz of bullets flying a little way overhead'. Better to stand in the shelter of a doorway, watching the looters 'pushing and pulling each other, till through broken windows all the treasures of India, Arabia and Samarkand were open before them'.[12]

Bessie and Mrs Gogan enter, the pride of a great joy illuminating their faces. Bessie is pushing the pram which is filled with clothes and boots; on the top of the boots and clothes is a fancy table, which Mrs Gogan is holding with her left hand, while with her right hand she holds a chair on the top of her head. They are heard talking to each other before they enter.

Mrs Gogan: I don't remember ever havin' seen such lovely pairs as them, with th' pointed toes an' the cuban heels.

Bessie: They'll go grand with th' dresses we're after liftin', an' when we've stitched a sthray bit o' silk to lift th' bodices a little higher, so as to shake th' shame out o' them, an' make them fit for women that hasn't lost themselves in th' nakedness o' th' times.

(*The Plough and the Stars*, Act 3)

Back home, British soldiers searched the house for snipers, and with the other men of the house Seán was rounded up to spend the night in St Barnabas Church.

Fluther: What sort of a church? Is it a Protestan' church?

Corporal Stoddart: I dunnow; I suppowse so.

Fluther (dismayed): Be God, it'll be a nice thing to be stuck all night in a Protestan' church.

Corporal Stoddart: Bring the cawds; you moight get a chance of a goime.

Fluther: Ah, no, that wouldn't . . . I wondher? (*After a moment's thought*) Ah, I don't think we'd be doin' anything derogatory be playin' cards in a Protestan' church.

(*Ibid*, Act 4)

In October 1917 O'Casey's first independently published work appeared as a broadside entitled *Thomas Ashe*. This was expanded in the following year and published in pamphlet form as *The Story*

of Thomas Ashe. (Later the title was changed to
[36] *The Sacrifice of Thomas Ashe.*) Ashe, a member of the Citizen Army and a friend of Seán's, was arrested in 1917 during a round-up of republican suspects. His death in prison after a lengthy hunger-strike during which he was forcibly fed, aroused considerable sorrow and anger and was partly instrumental in bringing about the change in public attitudes in favour of the 1916 rebels. Although Seán had by now severed his connection with the organisations that took part in the Easter Rising, this publication shows he was still committed to the cause of Irish independence, believing he could best serve it with his pen rather than his sword. It was probably on the strength of his first published work that the publishing firm of Maunsell & Co. commissioned him to write the story of the Irish Citizen Army.

Despite his breach with the Irish Citizen Army, Seán agreed to take upon himself the task of writing its history. This little book of some seventy-odd pages appeared in 1919 under the title of *The Story of the Irish Citizen Army*; the author's name, owing to a printer's error, appears as 'P. Ó Cathasaigh'. Its bias against James Connolly makes it of doubtful historical value. It drew strong criticism from members of the Citizen Army and thus further isolated Seán from his former colleagues. Its publication coincided with what must have been for him the greatest tragedy in his life so far, the death of his mother. After collecting his meagre cheque for £15 for delivering the manuscript, which he planned to offer as an earnest of his ability to pay the funeral expenses, he was brutally told by the undertaker that until he could get it cashed the funeral would not take place. For Seán, who had no bank account, this proved to be no easy task.

After his mother's death he found it impossible to

remain at 18 Abercorn Road with his brother Mick. Their widely differing political views led to frequent quarrels, and Mick, as O'Casey states in *Inishfallen Fare Thee Well*, was drinking heavily.[13] (It seems that both Tom and Mick were heavy drinkers, which may account for O'Casey's personal abstemiousness.) Now he would have to find somewhere else to live. Tom and Bella were both dead, and Isaac had emigrated to Liverpool. In January 1920 he moved to 35 Mountjoy Square, where he shared a room with a friend, Micheál Ó Maoláin. This was a time of terror. The warfare between the IRA and the police intensified, Dublin was under curfew, and dawn raids on houses by the notorious Black and Tans and Auxies (Auxiliary Division of the Royal Irish Constabulary), especially in the poorer districts of the city, were a frequent and frightening occurrence.

> Seán's eyes were closing and dimming, thoughts swooned faintly through his mind into the humming whine of motor-engines coming quick along the road outside. Up on his elbow he shot as he heard the sound of braking, telling him the lorries were outside the house, or those on either side. Then he shot down again to hide as a blinding beam from a searchlight poured through the window, skimming the cream of the darkness out of the room. It silvered the old walls for a few moments, then withdrew like a receding tide to send its beam on another part of the house. Then there was a volley of battering blows on the obstinate wooden door, mingled with the crash of falling glass that told Seán the panels on each side of it had been shattered by the hammer of a rifle-butt.[14]

The plot of *The Shadow of a Gunman* was being conceived. Soon after the raid he moved to a room of his own in 422 North Circular Road. Up to this,

he had only been able to get casual jobs as a builder's
[38] labourer; now he obtained work as a janitor at a house in Langrishe Place where Jim Larkin's sister, Delia Larkin, ran an entertainment called 'House Game', somewhat similar to the modern game of 'Bingo'. At the same time he acted as secretary of the Release Jim Larkin Committee, Larkin himself having been jailed for ten years in the United States for his involvement in labour troubles.

Estranged from his political contacts in Liberty Hall, Seán was for a time a rebel without a platform. However, he found consolation in 'a good-looking lass' training to be a schoolteacher, a girl with 'big hazel eyes', 'a heavy mass of rich brown hair, softly rounded chin, fine complexion, and full white throat'.[15] Seán met Maura Keating – the 'Nora Creena' of the autobiography – at the St Laurence O'Toole Dramatic Club in 1917. Now he was to find ways other than political pamphleteering to engage his urge to write. His love poems – some published in *Songs of the Wren*[16] and some many years later in *Windfalls*[17] – are marred by his tendency to strain after effect and indulge in purple passages. More successful are his lively satirical ballads set to traditional airs: 'The Devil's Recruitin' Campaign', 'The Man from the Daily Mail', 'The Demi-Semi Home Rule Bill' and 'The Constitutional Movement Must Go On'. The last of these was sung by Seán himself at a 'Concert and Play' organised in November 1917 by the O'Toole Club and performed in the Olympia Theatre to raise funds for 'Meals for Necessitous Children of the Poor'. In the play *Naboclish* (Never Mind It) Seán appeared as a dim-witted English tourist, a part singularly unsuited to his thick Dublin accent.

4

Gradually the hand of Providence was guiding him

closer to his ultimate goal. Barely a month later he visited the Abbey Theatre for the first time as a guest of some friends. The play he saw was *Blight: The Tragedy of Dublin* by Oliver St John Gogarty, writing under the pseudonym of 'Alpha and Omega'. It was a play that caused some stir, exposing as it did the horrific living conditions in the city's slums.

It seems likely that this first visit to the Abbey, coinciding with the production of Gogarty's slum play, was the final spur that urged him to write a play himself laid in an environment and peopled by characters he knew so well. Gabriel Fallon relates that, returning home one evening with Seán some eight or nine years later, they found themselves at a spot on the north side of the city known as the Five Lamps.

> 'Look, Gaby,' he said, 'it was here on this very spot that I got the idea that I was going to become a playwright, that I became determined to write plays.' 'One evening', he went on, 'Frank Cahill and I went to the Abbey. We strolled back and we stood here. "D'ye know," said I to Frank "that wasn't such a bad play we saw tonight." "Bedad, it wasn't," said Frank. "You, Seán, could write a far better play than that one." "D'ye really think so, Frank?" says I. "I'm bloody sure of it, Seán," said Frank. Well, Gaby, I pushed back me cap on me head, looked up at the sky an' said: "So help me God, Frank, I will!" '[18]

In the autumn of 1919 he submitted his first two plays to the Abbey, *The Frost in the Flower* and *The Harvest Festival*. The former was originally intended for production by the St Laurence O'Toole Club. It was turned down on the grounds that its satirical portrait of Frank Cahill and other members would give offence. *The Harvest Festival*, written around 1918–19, is the only one of his 'prentice' [40] plays to survive, though it was neither published nor produced during his lifetime. In action, theme, and characterisation it contains elements that were later incorporated in *Red Roses For Me* and *The Star Turns Red*. The plot revolves around the reaction of the middle-class Dublin Protestant community to a strike of the workers that resembles the 1913 lockout. The proletarian hero, Jack Rocliffe, like Ayamonn Breydon in *Red Roses* a Protestant and an idealised portrait of the playwright himself, is killed in the ensuing action. Refused burial within the precincts of his own church whose members object to his leftist views, his funeral service, like that of the hero of *The Star Turns Red*, is held in the Trades Union Hall.

The play was turned down by the Abbey mainly on the grounds of the stilted dialogue and stereotyped characterisation of the middle-class characters, 'as unreal as the "Stage Irishman of twenty years ago"'. However, in rejecting the play, along with *The Frost in the Flower*, the management added: 'We are sorry to return the plays for the author's work interests us, but we don't think either would succeed on the stage.'[19] The recent publication of *The Harvest Festival* (New York 1979) bears out this judgment.

His third assault upon the Abbey was *The Crimson in the Tri-Colour*, a play dealing with the struggle between Sinn Féin and Labour. This received a far more detailed criticism. Indeed, Lady Gregory was at one time in favour of staging it, despite its obvious faults, in order to give experience to a writer whose work she found promising. 'I believe there is something in you and your strong point is characterisation,' she wrote.[20] Yeats found the play 'loose' and 'vague', but pointed out that 'on the other hand it is so constructed that in every scene there is something for pit and gallery to cheer or boo'.[21] After a long delay, due to

Lennox Robinson having mislaid the manuscript, the play was turned down. Seán now showed a touch of the resentment that was to break out with such devastating effect when *The Silver Tassie* was rejected: 'I have re-read the work and find it as interesting as ever, in no way deserving the contemptuous dismissal it has received from the reader [Yeats] you have quoted.'[22]

Meanwhile in March 1922 he had submitted a one-act dramatisation of an allegorical tale he had contributed to the Republican weekly, *Poblacht na hÉireann*, entitled *The Seamless Coat of Cathleen.*[23] The Cathleen of the title is Cathleen Ni Houlihan, the personification of Ireland, and her 'Seamless Coat' refers to the nominal unity of the new Free State before the outbreak of the Civil War. But by this time the Civil War was daily looming nearer, and it is perhaps not surprising that in these circumstances the play was rejected as being 'too definite a piece of propaganda for us to do'.[24] Undeterred, he determined to make one more attempt to get a play accepted. Since his first plays were rejected he had made further visits to the Abbey. Joseph Holloway, the diarist of the Dublin theatre, records O'Casey telling him in 1923 that he had seen and liked Daniel Corkery's play *The Labour Leader*, produced in September 1919, dealing with Jim Larkin's leadership during the 1913 lockout,[25] and in his autobiography he admits to seeing a play based on a short story by James Stephens. This was a one-act comedy, *The Wooing of Julia Elizabeth*, produced in August 1920, once again a play whose action was set in a tenement building. Now he was ready to accept Lady Gregory's advice 'to cut out all expression of self and develop his peculiar gift for character drawing'.[26] In 1922 he sent a two-act play, *On the Run*, to the Abbey. It was immediately accepted under the title of *The Shadow of a Gunman*. Seán Ó Cathasaigh had at last become Seán O'Casey.

3
Seán O'Casey

1

It was the end of March 1923 when *The Shadow of a Gunman* went into rehearsal. The Civil War had not yet ended. No longer a struggle conducted on strictly military lines, it had degenerated into a guerilla war of attrition. Dublin's theatres were under the armed guard of soldiers of the pro-Treaty Provisional Government against the threat of reprisals by the anti-Treaty Republicans. It was no time for theatre-going. The Abbey, playing to near empty houses, was on the verge of bankruptcy. O'Casey's play was scheduled for four performances only – three nights and a matinée – after which the theatre was to close down until August. On the opening night, Thursday 12 April, the house was less than half full. Although the press reviews were generally favourable, they were scarcely enthusiastic. Yet, by the end of the week, for the first time for many years, it was 'standing room only'.

The Shadow of a Gunman is not a great play. Its action consists of a string of characters in largely unrelated incidents. Only at the end, when the raid on the house by the Auxies takes place, does the action become truly dramatic. The reasons for its perhaps unexpected success were immediately perceived by Lady Gregory. In her journal for 15 April 1923 she recorded that 'The play was an immense success, beautifully acted, all the political points taken up with delight by a big audience.'[1] Acting and politics were the two major ingredients for O'Casey's success, not only in this play, but in the two major plays that were to complete his Dublin trilogy – though politics were also to be the cause of the anger and indignation of a sizeable section of his audience. And if the play was 'beautifully acted', it was because O'Casey, following Lady Gregory's advice to concentrate on character, had supplied a company of mostly Dublin-bred players with the material from which great performances could be created.

Dublin, especially the poorer districts, was – and still is – rich in the diversity and individuality of its characters, as it is in the flow and idiosyncrasies of language. Through his commitment to the working class, O'Casey, more than any other writer of the time, was able to capture and immortalise the essence of this living reality. Gabriel Fallon, himself a true-born Dubliner, recorded his first encounter with O'Casey's dialogue as he stepped onto the stage for the first rehearsal of the play: 'As I reached stage level my ear caught some of the richest Dublin dialogue I had ever heard, at least on the stage of the Abbey Theatre. It was spoken by F. J. McCormick with the proud consciousness of origin that marks the true-born Dubliner.'[2]

Besides the language and the bubbling earthy humour that O'Casey knew so well how to mix with tragedy, there was the play's identification with the current mood of disillusionment. In his study of O'Casey's political development Desmond Greaves has pointed out that in this play 'O'Casey presents the events of 1921. But he informs them with the atmosphere of 1922.'[3] When Donal Davoren, a character largely based on the playwright himself, asks: 'Are we ever going to know what peace and security are?', or his room-mate, Séamus Shields, complains that instead of the gunmen dying for the people, it's the people dying for the gunmen, they are voicing what most citizens felt when what was in 1921 a heroic struggle for independence against the might of Britain had turned in 1922 into the horror of fratricidal strife. In a world torn by violence the disillusionment that O'Casey voices is not confined to Ireland alone. Lady Gregory in her advice to O'Casey had also urged him to give up writing about ideas. This he never did. Had he ceased to speak out fearlessly those things he felt and believed, he would have been a richer man but a poorer playwright.

Those four performances of his play did not make O'Casey's fortune. The royalties amounted to £4, and he had to wait for this pittance until the Abbey – in serious trouble with the bank – was in a position to issue a cheque. So Seán had to continue to earn his livelihood as a builder's labourer. But when the theatre opened again in August it was with his play once again filling the house to capacity, and he knew that his true vocation was within his reach.

From now on the budding dramatist visited the Abbey regularly and, what was more important for his future development, the performances of the Dublin Drama League. Founded in 1918, largely on Lennox Robinson's initiative, the Drama League performed on Sunday and Monday nights in the Abbey, introducing the works of contemporary continental and American playwrights. Among the plays admired by O'Casey were those of the German Expressionist school.

In September 1923 his one-act play *Kathleen Listens In*, 'a political phantasy', was accepted for production. It made use of expressionist techniques by introducing typed characters such as the Free Stater, the Republican, the Farmer, a Labourer, representatives of the various factions and political parties vying for power in the newly born state. The Kathleen of the title was, of course, Ireland itself;

'Listens In' refers to listening to the new invention of radio. Gabriel Fallon recalls: 'Gradually it dawned upon some of us that we were taking part in a piece of blistering satire directed against everything and almost every one in the infant State.'[4] When the play opened on 1 October 1923, along with Lady Gregory's *The Rising of the Moon* and Shaw's *The Man of Destiny*, the laughter was restrained ('hardly more than ten per cent of the audience laughed together') and the curtain fell with 'a few dispirited handclaps obviously intended for the players'.[5]

Seán had submitted another one-act play at the same time as *Kathleen Listens In*. This was *The Cooing of Doves*. Much to his disappointment, this was turned down in favour of his 'political phantasy'. It was 'full of wild discussion and rows in a public house', later to be used as the basis for the second act of *The Plough and the Stars*. Neither play was chosen by him for inclusion in his collected works, and the typed copy of *The Cooing of Doves* was destroyed in the Abbey fire in 1951.

Undeterred by the failure of his one-act play, Seán now 'swore an oath that he would write a play that would be such that the Abbey would not be big enough to hold the audience that would want to see it'.[6]

2

'On a little by-road, out beyant Finglas, he was found.' 'Surely' wrote Gabriel Fallon, 'this is the most intriguing, the most interest-catching opening line in the history of modern drama.'[7] Indeed, it might serve as the perfect illustration of a basic precept for all would-be playwrights. Seán had learned the lesson that failure and persistence teach, but which only the blinding flashes of inspiration can raise above the worthy, the commonplace and the purely popular.

He had set out to write a tragedy of the Civil War in
[46] which a young Free State soldier, Johnny Boyle, crippled by a 'bullet he got in the hip in Easter Week' and 'the bomb that shattered his arm in the fight in O'Connell Street', betrayed his neighbour, a Republican 'Irregular', and 'sent him to his grave'. In fact the play turned out to be far more than this – more even than the tragi-comedy of the Boyle family: Johnny's pregnant sister abandoned by her lover, his heroic mother, Juno, and his strutting 'paycock' of a father, the bogus 'Captain' Boyle, and his parasitic 'butty', Joxer Daly. *Juno and the Paycock*, by some acclaimed as O'Casey's greatest play, has become part of the eternal message of humanity: the tears and laughter that make men so much greater than the angels.

The play opened at the Abbey on 3 March 1924 with a production immortalised in the theatre's history by the performances of Sara Allgood (Juno), Barry Fitzgerald (Captain Boyle) and F. J. McCormick (Joxer Daly), supported by a company unrivalled for its ability to capture not only the language but the authentic essence of O'Casey's Dubliners. If the playwright gave much to the players, the players gave much to the playwright. Here again was the perfect communion between author and performers that Yeats and his fellow-writers had sought in founding the National Theatre. The tragedy was that this communion was so soon to be broken – and by O'Casey himself. Meanwhile *Juno and the Paycock* became the most popular play in the Abbey's repertoire. For the first time in the theatre's history the directors were compelled to keep it running for two weeks, which was at that time contrary to the Abbey's policy. Through the years 1924–25 repeated performances of the play were to save the Abbey from bankruptcy.

When it first appeared, *Juno* was not without its

critics. There were those who considered its mixture of tragedy and comedy unacceptable, even declaring that the superbly ironic last scene between the drunken Boyle and the equally inebriated Joxer should be cut. Some condemned the play on moral grounds, claiming that the pregnancy of an unmarried girl was a most improper subject for dramatic presentation. When the play was presented in Cork the management of the theatre insisted that reference to Mary Boyle's condition be suppressed. More ominous for the future were the strictures of those nationalists who objected to what they considered to be the unfavourable portrayal of Irish men and women in the struggle for national independence.

In the meantime Seán had found a close friend in Lady Gregory. His attachment to her lasted throughout his life, despite the sad breach in their relationship that followed the rejection of *The Silver Tassie*. In June 1924 he accepted her invitation to spend the first of his visits to her beautiful home, Coole Park, in Co. Galway. It was a visit he idealised in the chapter entitled 'Where Wild Swans Nest' in *Inishfallen Fare Thee Well.*

Now at last he could give up the pick and shovel and call himself a professional writer. In Dublin he had become something of a literary lion, invited to gatherings at Yeats's house in Merrion Square and frequenting the 'at homes' of AE (George Russell). In August the London publishing house of Macmillan was arranging to publish *Juno and the Paycock* and *The Shadow of a Gunman*, and in February of the following year he sent the book, dedicated 'To Maura [Keating] and the Abbey Theatre', to Lady Gregory with 'the proud vision of the little volume expanding itself in the company of superior associations in the great library of Coole'.[8]

In the meantime another one-act play opened at the

Abbey. This was *Nannie's Night Out* (29 September
[48] 1924), mistakenly referred to by Lady Gregory in her journal as *Lizzie's Night Out*. In this short sketch Sara Allgood gave a memorable performance as Spunker, a meths-drinker on her first night out of prison. In Seán's original script she was shot while tackling a gunman, but for some reason best known to themselves Yeats and Robinson insisted on Seán changing this to her arrest by the police. Once again there were ominous signs of the opposition that was building up against the playwright. This time it came from the Gaelic enthusiasts. A remark, made by one of the characters referring to a crippled boy from the slums, that 'the Government might be better employed in putting food in the young lad's stomach than in stuffing the Irish language down his throat', earned Seán his first hisses from a section of the audience – an ominous foretaste of the reception that was to greet his next play.

In August 1925, while Seán was putting the finishing touches to his new play – a play that was to elicit a response far more hostile than the wild hisses of *Nannie's Night Out* – an incident occurred that brought his close association with the Abbey players to an abrupt conclusion. On 10 August he attended the first night of Shaw's *Man and Superman* at the Abbey. He considered the performance to be 'bad in every way'. When the curtain fell he marched backstage and tactlessly voiced his criticism to the play's director, M. J. Dolan. Dolan was no friend of O'Casey's. He promptly relayed these criticisms to the leading player, F. J. McCormick. A flaming row ensued. Undeterred, Seán followed this up with a letter setting forth his criticism in no uncertain terms and challenging Dolan to publicise it. Some nights later Seán was crossing the Abbey stage to join the actors in the Green Room when he was stopped by Seán Barlow, the theatre carpenter and painter.

Barlow: May I ask what you're doin' on th' stage?
Sean: I'm on my way to the Green Room.
Barlow: There's none but the actors and officials allowed on the stage, and we'd be glad if you came this way no more.

He turned away, leaving the other Seán victor on the field, and never after set a foot, either on the Abbey stage, or in the Green Room.[9]

In September his new play, *The Plough and the Stars*, was accepted for production. But already Providence, or Fate, was edging him towards a world elsewhere. In the following month J. B. Fagan, actor-manager and playwright, was seeking the Abbey's permission for a London production of *Juno and the Paycock*, and on 16 November it opened at the Royalty Theatre to an enthusiastic press with a cast including Sara Allgood as Juno, Arthur Sinclair as Captain Boyle, and Sydney Morgan as Joxer Daly. Seán O'Casey's 'apotheosis' had begun, but a valuable relationship had been lost.

3

From the beginning it was evident that *The Plough and the Stars* was going to cause trouble. M. J. Dolan, who combined the jobs of manager and play director, wrote to Lady Gregory after reading the script:

> At any time I would think twice about having anything to do with it. The language in it is – to use an Abbey phrase – beyond the beyonds. The song at the end of the second act, sung by the girl-in-the-streets, is unpardonable.[10]

Prompted as much by his dislike of O'Casey as by his distaste for the play, Dolan urged Dr George O'Brien, the government nominee on the board of directors, to take action. O'Brien, who laid no claim to being a literary or dramatic critic, had already given his [50] official approval to the play, but he now took fright and demanded considerable changes in the script. The love scene in the first act between Jack Clitheroe and Nora 'does not ring true', he declared; the part of Rosie Redmond, the prostitute, 'could not possibly be allowed to stand'; the song 'I once had a lover a tailor, but he could do nothing for me' was 'outrageous'. There were numerous words and phrases, some of which he listed, that must be changed; failing this, he feared there would be a public outcry, and the government subsidy might be withdrawn. Yeats and his fellow-directors conceded that the love scene contained passages that did not ring true. (There were indeed such mawkish endearments as 'little rogue of the white breast'.) Reluctantly they also agreed to the removal of the song. Beyond this they would not go. Lady Gregory declared: 'If we have to choose between the subsidy and our freedom, it is our freedom we choose.'[11]

The ill omens continued. Strong differences arose between Seán and Lennox Robinson over the casting of the play. Gabriel Fallon goes so far as to state that 'Consciously or unconsciously Robinson was out to damage O'Casey's play.'[12] The row over Seán's earlier criticism of the performance of *Man and Superman* had left its mark on the attitude of many of the players. Rehearsals were conducted in an atmosphere of tension and mistrust between the pro- and anti-O'Casey parties. Eileen Crowe, who was cast as Mrs Gogan, refused to play the part unless it was agreed to remove the line 'Any kid, livin' or dead, that Jinnie Gogan had since [her marriage] was got between th' border o' the Ten Commandments.' She was replaced by another actress. There were ugly scenes between Seán and F. J. McCormick over the word 'snotty'. Ria Mooney related that members of the company tried to discourage her from playing the part of the prostitute. O'Casey threatened to withdraw the play rather than give way to a 'Vigilance Committee of the actors'.[13] Meanwhile rumours were circulating in Dublin that he had written the most immoral play yet. As a result, the house was booked out for the first night (8 February 1926), and as Holloway reported,

> There was electricity in the air before and behind the curtains at the Abbey tonight when Seán O'Casey's play *The Plough and the Stars* was first produced. The theatre was thronged with distinguished people and before the door opened the queue to pit entrance extended past old Abbey Street – not a quarter of them got in.[14]

If O'Casey's enemies expected a hostile reception, they must have been disappointed. The applause was generous, the press favourable. The *Irish Independent* predicted that the play would 'prove to be the most popular of Mr O'Casey's works'. But the nationalists were not likely to condone what they considered a 'studied insult to the men of the 1916 Rising, and an outrage perpetrated on the banners of the Citizen Army and the Volunteers'. On Tuesday and Wednesday there was a certain amount of hissing. On Thursday the notorious riot took place. It was clearly a planned demonstration. The stage was stormed, speeches of protest were made, stink-bombs fouled the air, the police were called in, and Yeats, in his element, thundered from the stage with upraised arm:

> You have disgraced yourselves again. Is this to be an ever recurring celebration of the arrival of Irish genius? Synge first and then O'Casey. The news of the happening of the last few minutes will go from country to country. Dublin has rocked the cradle of genius. From such a scene in this theatre went forth

> the fame of Synge. Equally the fame of O'Casey is
> [52] born here tonight. This is his apotheosis.[15]

Not a word of this could be heard above the uproar, but Yeats, a master of publicity who must have had prior knowledge of the demonstration, had already taken the precaution of handing a copy of his speech to the *Irish Times*. Thereafter the play was performed with plain-clothes police lining the walls of the auditorium.

A stranger to Ireland and her tumultuous history might well ask why *The Plough and the Stars* caused such an indignant reaction whereas *Juno and the Paycock*, in which the male characters are conspicuously lazy and cowardly, was generally applauded by the audience. The answer lies partly in the political backgrounds of the two plays and the consequent emotional overtones to which those backgrounds gave rise.

In *Juno* the background is the Civil War. Mrs Tancred's anguished cry as she goes to attend her son's funeral, a cry reiterated by Juno when she too loses her son:

> Sacred Heart of the Crucified Jesus, take away our hearts o' stone . . . an' give us hearts of flesh. . . . Take away this murderin' hate . . . an' give us Thine own eternal love!

is a message with which, after the senseless fratricide of the Civil War, the great majority of Irish people would agree.

In *The Plough* the background is the Easter Rising of 1916; an event that had assumed a semi-legendary, semi-religious significance. The 'blood sacrifice' of Pádraic Pearse, James Connolly and the other leaders had become the symbol of Ireland's age-long struggle for freedom. It was both a crucifixion and a resurrection. By depicting the participants, not as heroes but as human beings subject to the fears, the pomps and vanities of the flesh, and by showing the ordinary Dubliners as indifferent, or hostile, or having a glorious jamboree pillaging the shops, the play seemed to ardent patriots, especially those whose menfolk had perished in the event, to be a deliberate attempt to debunk the spirit that had inspired and uplifted those who took part.

Moreover, in *Juno*, the plot of which concerns the false expectations and pretentions of the Boyle family arising from the misinterpretation of a relative's will, the motivation is social and domestic. Any objections raised by its critics were on moral grounds. In *The Plough* it is the Rising that motivates the action. Nora's outcry against her husband's participation in it becomes a condemnation of the Rising itself. In *The Plough* there are no heroes, only victims.

At the end of the second week's run a public meeting was called to discuss the play. Seán attended, though his decision to do so was probably unwise, for the tension of the past weeks had taken its toll of his health. After a few words he was overcome by giddiness and forced to sit down. This was later ascribed, most unfairly, to 'lack of guts'. Opening the case against the play was Mrs Hannah Sheehy-Skeffington, the widow of the patriot and pacifist executed in 1916 whom Seán had praised in *The Story of the Irish Citizen Army*. Hers was a fair but hard-hitting attack on what she considered was a totally unjust picture of the men of 1916. 'There is not a single gleam of heroism throughout,' she declared. When Seán felt able to rise again he replied that he was not trying to write about heroes but about the people he knew and the life he knew. He then turned upon his enemies. 'He mocked them, laughed at them, ridiculed them, using every weapon in his armoury to pierce their pompous patriotism.'[16] But in the event this did little to help his case.

Seán left the meeting 'weary and scornful of the
[54] end of it all'. He had suffered and striven to earn his place as an Abbey playwright; now in the moment of his 'apotheosis' it had turned sour on him. The actors had banned him from their company. His fellow-writers Liam O'Flaherty, F. R. Higgins, R. M. Fox and Austin Clarke were busy denouncing him and his plays in the *Irish Statesman*. The girl he loved was not prepared to stand out against her Catholic parents in their disapproval of him. The Irish Transport and General Workers' Union had gone soft under the leadership of William O'Brien, and his old comrades of the Labour movement were alienated by his criticisms. It was time for him to go.

> If he stayed in Dublin life would be embarrassing to meet. Dublin was too close to everyone. All its streets led into the one square where everyone met, where hands were shaken, shoulders clapped, and drinks taken to every other person's health. Sound and happy association, with one reservation – that when one was on the way to a good creation, he might be waylaid, left by the wayside, to die there, unfortified by the rites of the Church.[17]

Like his contemporary James Joyce, he 'would not serve', so now he must find a world elsewhere. But where? By living in the country, or by crossing over to England? If he chose the country,

> He'd still be confined within the kin and den of Cosgravian and De Valerian politics and well within the sphere and influence of Irish rosaries, Anthony's Annals, and all the crowding rolipoli-holiness of the Pope's green island: with Church of Ireland stained-glass windows shining timidly through the mist that does be on the bog.[18]

In London he had just been awarded the Hawthornden Prize of £100 for 'the best work of imaginative literature published in the last twelve months'. [55] The prize was to be presented by the Earl of Oxford and Asquith, the Liberal statesman and former Prime Minister, a fervent admirer of *Juno and the Paycock*. Should he go? And then, if he did go, would he want to come back? It was when he returned from that ineffective debate on *The Plough* that Seán found a telegram waiting for him from J. B. Fagan. *Juno and the Paycock* was to transfer from the Royalty to the Fortune Theatre. Its chances of surviving the change would be greatly strengthened if O'Casey would come to London. So on 5 March 1926 he packed his few personal needs, including his best suit, and left.

4
Exile in London

1

Despite what he tells us in the final chapter of *Inishfallen Fare Thee Well*, Seán had not decided at this point to leave Dublin for ever. He neither gave up his room in 422 North Circular Road, nor made arrangements for his books and other effects to follow after him. In an interview with a reporter from the *Daily Sketch* (24 March) he said that although he liked London and the English, he could not live there and would soon be returning to Dublin to work.

On his arrival in London he was met by J. B. Fagan and his wife, and on the following day he was introduced to the press. Fagan well knew that in Seán he had a priceless publicity asset. The 'ex-labourer genius' with the cloth cap, red muffler and trench coat, the 'slum dramatist' with his thick Dublin accent and his outspoken views was a reporter's dream. He was interviewed by the BBC and by nearly every newspaper, magazine and periodical in the country.

> He was photographed in the theatre and in the flat where he lived, photographed talking to policemen; brought face to face with those whose pencils could dash down a swift impression to appear fresh and full-blown in some paper the following day. . . . He was tired of it before it had well begun . . . for Seán in his heart didn't care a damn what anyone thought of him.[1]

The publicity he attracted gave *Juno and the Pay-*

cock new life when on 8 March 1926 it opened at the Fortune Theatre. To the royalties he was receiving from the London production were added those from New York, where *Juno* opened at the Mayfair Theatre on 15 March to be favourably received by one of New York's leading critics, George Jean Nathan. Later Nathan was to become one of O'Casey's greatest admirers and friends.

In London Seán was visiting the art galleries and seeing as many dramatic productions as he could. He had little good to say about the fashionable playwrights Noël Coward, Edgar Wallace and R. C. Sherriff, but there was Kommisarjevsky's great production of *The Three Sisters* at the Barnes Theatre, Sir Barry Jackson's presentation of *The Marvellous History of St Bernard** by Henri Ghéon, and *The Immortal Hour*, to which he was taken by Lady Londonderry. The Londonderrys were among his new friends; and Seán, sticking rigidly to his sartorial style of grey suit, black and yellow St Laurence O'Toole Club tie, and his variegated jumper, became a centre of attraction at their 'at homes', Lady Londonderry tactfully arranging for him to be served with a pot of tea in a side-room. Other fashionable hostesses also sought his presence at their receptions. But, as he wrote to Gabriel Fallon, 'This is a lonely city after all. I wish sometimes I was singing "Goodbye Piccadilly, Farewell Leicester Square" for they're so damned busy here, they haven't time for friends.'[2]

Nevertheless, he was making new friends: Sybil Thorndike, 'a very natural, kind and lovable woman'; Bernard Shaw, as much an idol to Seán as Jim Larkin himself; Augustus John, who was to paint a fine portrait of him; and William (Billy) McElroy. McElroy had made a small fortune by processing coal from the

* O'Casey wrongly refers to this play in *Rose and Crown* as *The Marvellous Adventures of St Bernard.*

slag heaps for boiler fuel, a genial soul who loved [58] nothing better than a flutter on the horses or on a new play. He had already backed *Juno* and *The Plough* and was to be one of the backers for Seán's next play, *The Silver Tassie*.

2

For some time now, perhaps dating back to his meeting the wounded soldiers in St Vincent's Hospital, he had been trying to get to grips with a play about the Great War, but the essential pivot to the action was missing. He found it in McElroy's dull and dusty office. The miners were on strike, and business was at a standstill. McElroy was sitting at his desk humming a tune when Seán entered.

> Then the hum changed to a whistle, then words began to trickle through it to an air Seán had never heard before. He cocked an ear to listen. . . .
>
> Gae bring to me a pint of wine,
> And fill it in a silver tassie;
> That I may drink before I go,
> A service to my bonnie lassie.
>
> The boat rocks at the pier o' Leith,
> Full loud the wind blows from the ferry
> The ship rides at the Berwick Law,
> An' I must leave my bonnie Mary!
>
> The trumpets sound, the banners fly,
> The glittering spears are ranked ready;
> The shouts of war are heard afar,
> The battle closes thick and bloody.
>
> It's not the roar of sea or shore,
> That makes me longer wish to tarry,
> Nor shouts of war that's heard afar –
> It's leaving thee, my bonnie lassie!

> . . . Seán was startled. Aaron's rod had budded. He hummed it in his tiny flat in South Kensington. He hummed it in the dead of night, strolling down the Cromwell Road. He would give the title of the song to his next play.[3]

The words written by Robert Burns provided Seán with the spring from which *The Silver Tassie*'s plot leapt into life: a toast, pledged to his love by a warrior before taking ship to the war. In the first act we see Harry Heegan, 'who on the football field could crash a twelve-stone flyer off his feet', returning victorious from the match, where his prowess has won for his club the silver cup. His leave from the front is now up; and he, with his ferocious neighbour Teddy Foran and his mate Barney Bagnall, must hasten to the boat that is to carry them back to the trenches. Before they go they take a final drink from the victory cup.

> *Harry:* The song that the little Jock used to sing, Barney, what was it? The little Jock we left shrivellin' on the wire after the last push?
>
> *Barney:* "Will ye no come back again"?
>
> *Harry:* No, no, the one we all used to sing with him, "The Silver Tassie".

Seán remembered his talks with the wounded soldiers during his sojourn in St Vincent's Hospital. This was the setting he chose for his third act, in which Harry, maimed for life, is deserted by his girl friend, Jessie Taite, who is now bent on flirting with Barney Bagnall, the glorious possessor of the Victoria Cross. But how was he to show the Great War itself? For this he needed a larger canvas than the one he had used for the 1916 Rising. Naturalism was not enough; he would use the expressionist techniques he had observed in the plays of Strindberg and others in the productions of the Dublin Drama League. In his great war scene, one of the finest in dramatic

literature, with its ruined monastery, its broken
[60] crucifix and its great howitzer gun, Seán used chanting based on the Catholic Mass (thereby unwittingly incurring the anathema of the Church when the play was eventually produced in Dublin), while the hymn to the gun that comes as a climax to the second act –

> Hail cool-hardened tower of steel embossed
> With the fever'd, figment thought of man;
> Guardian of our love and hate and fear,
> Speak for us to the inner-ear of God! –

seems to have been inspired by Wilfred Owen's war poem 'On Seeing a Piece of Our Artillery Brought into Action':

> Be slowly lifted up, thou long black arm,
> Great gun towering toward heaven,
> about to curse;
> Sway steep against them, and for years
> rehearse
> Huge imprecations like a blasting
> charm. . . .[4]

In placing this second act in the war zone Seán was also to incur the censure of Yeats. 'You are not interested in the Great War; you never stood on its battle fields or walked its hospitals,' wrote Yeats.[5] Seán's reply was deadly: 'Was Shakespeare at Actium or Phillipi? Was G. B. Shaw in the boats with the French, or in the forts with the British when St Joan and Dunois made the attack that relieved Orleans? And someone I think wrote a poem about Tír na nÓg who never took a header into the land of youth.'[6]

The rejection of the play by the Abbey was one of the reasons why Seán was to make his final break with his native land; but there was another. In October 1926 he concluded a letter to Gabriel Fallon with 'Not married, nor any intention of marrying yet.'[7]

He was, however, seeing a lot of a pretty young Irish-born actress named Eileen Carey.

Seán first met Eileen towards the end of April in Fagan's office at the Fortune Theatre. Fagan had decided to replace *Juno and the Paycock* with *The Plough and the Stars*, using most of the cast of the former play. Eileen had just returned from understudying and playing a small part in a United States tour of George M. Cohan's play *American Born*. In New York she read *Juno* with 'astonishment, delight and awe'. She returned to London with a burning desire to meet its author. From their first meeting it was clear that Seán and Eileen were interested in each other. A few days later Fagan called her back to the theatre. Kathleen O'Regan, who was due to play the important part of Nora Clitheroe in *The Plough*, was ill; rehearsals had begun; and the play was to open on 12 May. Eileen, with very limited stage experience, entirely confined to musical comedy, was to audition for the part.

> As always the prospect of an audition scared me; I still had sciatica and had to be doped to blur the pain. Yet Seán was so bent on having me that I got through the part with him – and in front of Fagan – and they arranged for me to be coached, as Kathleen O'Regan had been, by the veteran actress Kate Rorke.[8]

In June the play transferred to the New Theatre, where Kathleen O'Regan returned to the part of Nora Clitheroe, and Eileen was eventually to find work in a tour of *The Street Singer*, a musical comedy with a libretto by Frederick Lonsdale.

3

In the meantime Seán had made up his mind about his immediate future. He would stay in London – at

any rate for the next three years. In an interview with
[62] a correspondent of the *Daily Sketch* dated 7 July, he said:

> I like London and London likes me. That's more than I can say of Ireland. I have a good deal of courage, but not much patience, and it takes both courage and patience to live in Ireland. The Irish have no time for those who do not agree with their ideas, and I have no time for those who don't agree with mine.

He had taken a three-year lease of a flat in 32 Clareville Street, Kensington, and on 16 July he returned to Dublin to collect his books and dispose of his furniture.

From now on Seán became heavily involved in a variety of projects, and progress on *The Silver Tassie* was slow. *The Plough* was published, and requests for translation rights were coming in from Russia, Sweden and Germany. He had broken his association with Fagan and had to arrange for the transfer to the New Theatre himself. There was a tour of *Juno* to the provincial cities to be arranged when *The Plough* finished its run in September. There were negotiations for a New York production of the play and for a London production of *The Shadow of a Gunman*. The latter play opened at the Court Theatre on 27 May 1927 under Sir Barry Jackson's management, coupled with Synge's one-act play *Riders to the Sea.* Once again he was able to use his Irish cast – Arthur Sinclair as Séamus Shields, Sara Allgood and Máire O'Neill as Mrs Henderson and Mrs Gallagher, and, to Seán's delight, Eileen Carey as the heroic girl, Minnie Powell, whose life is sacrificed to save the poet and supposed gunman, Donal Davoren, played by Harry Hutchinson.

The play ran for two months. Britain was still suffering from the effects of the general strike, and theatre business was poor. On 14 September Seán wrote to Gabriel Fallon that he was starting on the third act of *The Silver Tassie*. 'Besides I've been "keeping company" with a pretty girl and she has at times pushed my thought away from the play. The two of us may possibly go over to Dublin soon.'

Seán O'Casey and Eileen Carey were married in the Catholic Church of all Souls and the Redeemer on 23 September 1927. Billy McElroy was best man, and the married couple left for a honeymoon in Ireland, staying first in Howth and later in Dublin itself.

In Dublin much time was spent in visiting Seán's 'butties', in particular Gabriel Fallon, Barry Fitzgerald ('Will' Shields), one of the few Abbey actors who remained a loyal friend, and Dr J. D. Cummins, Seán's eye specialist. There were visits to the Abbey, and Seán wanted Eileen to see all his favourite haunts in the city that he both loved and castigated. Eileen, though born in Dublin, had been brought up and educated in London.

When they returned to London Seán proudly brought Eileen to meet the Shaws, Augustus John and the Londonderrys. For a time they lived in Seán's two-roomed flat. Eileen was pregnant, and Billy McElroy persuaded them to look for a small house. *The Plough* had opened at the Hudson Theatre, New York, on 28 November, and now that *The Silver Tassie* was nearing completion, the financial situation seemed reasonably assured. The New York production was directed by Arthur Sinclair and included most of the Irish cast from London with the addition of Shelah Richards as Nora Clitheroe, the part she played in the original Dublin production. Another newcomer was Michael Scott, a young actor and architect who in time to come was to design the new Abbey Theatre. The play received mixed notices and only ran for thirty-two performances followed by a short tour. Seán's admirers in the United States were, however, steadily increasing, among them Eugene O'Neill and [64] the influential critics George Jean Nathan and Brooks Atkinson.

In February 1928 the O'Caseys moved to 19 Woronzow Road, St John's Wood, a small Georgian house with a pleasant little garden. Carpets, curtains, pictures and furniture had still to be found. As Eileen confesses, 'I had no sense of money at all, my taste being far beyond my means,' while Seán, anxious that Eileen should have a real home was 'supremely unconscious of price'.[9] The lease of the house was for ten years, and the preliminary deposit alone swallowed up nearly all the money they possessed. Everything now depended on *The Silver Tassie*.

4

On 17 March he sent the play to the Abbey, at the same time writing to Lady Gregory: 'Personally I think it is the best work I have done. I have certainly put my best into it, and have written the work solely because of love and a deep feeling that what I have written should be written.'[10] An ominous silence ensued. Seán was busy correcting proofs, for the play was to be published in June. C. B. Cochran, then at the height of his career as the leading London manager, read it, liked it, and was ready to buy the rights for a West End production. Billy McElroy had named one of his race-horses Silver Tassie and was prepared to be one of the play's backers. The prospects looked good.

Meanwhile at Woronzow Road Eileen's pregnancy was nearing its conclusion. A nurse had been engaged, and they had the benefit of Mrs Earle, Eileen's theatre dresser, to look after the housekeeping. There was some anxiety about the birth, and Eileen received little comfort from her mother, who warned her to be prepared for the possibility of the child being mentally afflicted since (so she said) Eileen's father had been unbalanced and the child's father was eccentric.

On 30 April the O'Caseys' first son, Breon, was born. Seán, on the gynaecologist's advice, had been sent away to spend the night with a friend. A telephone call in the morning brought him hurrying back to Woronzow Road. He was excited about the baby and longing to share his joy with Eileen. On the hall table was an envelope bearing the Abbey crest – Queen Maeve and her wolfhound. Here was surely the good news at last. He tore it open. The Abbey had rejected *The Silver Tassie*. Seán went upstairs, embraced Eileen and 'kept the Abbey refusal to himself, doing nothing to damage the wonderful, serene morning with the lilac trees in bloom beyond my window'.[11]

In order to 'soften the blow' Yeats had asked Lady Gregory to write to Seán herself enclosing his letter to Seán criticising the play. 'I woke early', she wrote, '(having got to sleep late – and really suffering at what I have had to write and send on.)'[12] Then she made a fatal mistake. In the belief that Seán would wish to have a totally honest report of the directors' views, she enclosed Lennox Robinson's criticism, together with two letters from Yeats which were not intended to be seen by the author.

> Believing it is right you should at once know what he [Yeats] – what we all – feel and think – I won't make any more comment – I know you will prefer this to any attempt to 'soften' things and will believe that I, we all – feel you would rather have the exact truth than evasion.[13]

The hesitations are an indication of her uncertainty as to the rightness of the decision to reject the play.

She had, at one stage of the arguments for and against
[66] the play, been against its outright rejection. Far more than either Robinson or Yeats, Lady Gregory, as a woman, was aware of Seán's sensitivity at this point in his career to the rejection of his work. Yeats, with his Olympian attitudes to his fellow-writers, could scarcely have realised what he was taking on in making his criticisms of *The Silver Tassie*, for Seán was not merely a master of invective, but in the cut and thrust of literary debate his wit was keener, his attacks more devastating and their sting more vicious than the magisterial pronouncements of Ireland's senior poet. Seán was not merely bitter about Yeats's rejection; he was, as he told David Krause many years later, 'bloody mad at him'. The verdict of the Nobel Prize winner that *The Silver Tassie* was a 'bad play' could effectively deprive it of its London and New York performance. There was only one way open to him – to fight the man himself.

Yeats's suggestion in his letter to Lady Gregory, dated 25 April, that Seán could let it be known to the press that he wished to 'withdraw the play for revision' and thus save himself the humiliation of an outright rejection – and, incidentally, relieve Yeats and his fellow-directors from the onus of turning it down – was the signal for Seán's attack. He wrote to Lennox Robinson:

> There is going to be no damned secrecy with me surrounding the Abbey's rejection of the play. Does he [Yeats] think that I would practice in my life the prevarications and wretchednesses that I laugh at in my plays? . . . Any journalist, Irish or English, who asks me about the Abbey production will be told that the play has been refused by the Abbey because they thought it a bad play, supplemented by me saying that I believe the play was refused because it was a good one.[14]

Seán took the letters concerning the criticisms of his play to Cochran and Daniel Macmillan, offering them the opportunity to withdraw the play from publication and production. Both stood by their own judgments. *The Silver Tassie* was published on 12 June, but it was over a year before Cochran was in a position to present it on the stage.

Meanwhile Seán sent all the letters, together with his blistering replies, to the *Irish Statesman* and the London *Observer.* AE (George Russell), the editor of the *Irish Statesman*, refused to publish them without the consent of the writers. The main ones appeared for the first time on Sunday 3 June in *The Observer* and were reprinted in the *Irish Times* on the following morning. Yeats wrote to the Society of Authors inquiring about the possibility of legal action. The letters were not written for publication, and this, he suggested, was a breach of copyright. He decided, however, that the better course would be to authorise the *Irish Statesman* to print all the letters, together with a criticism he had since received from Dr Walter Starkie, the government representative on the Abbey Theatre's board of directors, who was in Spain at the time of the rejection. On his return Starkie read the play and wrote that, in spite of his many criticisms of it, it should have been produced. This gave Seán the chance to dispose of Starkie's objections after he had finished with Yeats. As for Robinson, he was merely the 'Duke's Esquire', worth 'no more than a passing hurried thought'. But in his hard-hitting onslaught against the Abbey directors he was careful to avoid attacking Lady Gregory.

On 19 June Bernard Shaw weighed in heavily on O'Casey's side: 'What a hell of a play.... Of course the Abbey should have produced it.' At the same time he wrote to Lady Gregory:

Why do you and W. B. Y. treat O'Casey as a baby?

> Starkie was right, you should have done the play
> [68] anyhow. Seán is now *hors concours*. It is literally a hell of a play; but it will clearly force its way onto the stage, and Yeats should have submitted to it as a calamity imposed on him by the Act of God, if he could not welcome it as another *Juno*.[15]

The verbal duel between O'Casey and his critics echoed in the European and American press. Those who had never heard of either O'Casey or Yeats now learned about them for the first time.

Further bitterness between Seán and the Abbey directorate arose over the latter's attempt to prevent Arthur Sinclair and his Irish Players from presenting *Juno* and *The Plough* in Belfast, claiming that the National Theatre Society had the sole rights to present these plays in Ireland. The argument hinged on whether or not the society had given the required notice to renew their options on the plays for a further year. Seán denied that such notice of intention had been given, pointing out that the Abbey had made no attempt to tour the plays to Belfast until Sinclair announced his intention of doing so. A compromise was eventually reached with Lady Gregory's help, whereby the Abbey retained the right to present the plays in Dublin and Sinclair was permitted to produce them in Cork and Belfast.

On 12 September 1928 the contract for the London production of *The Silver Tassie* was signed, but until the royalties came in the financial situation was going to be difficult. Seán and Eileen were living far beyond their means, and unless *The Silver Tassie* could retrieve the situation, they would no longer be able to afford their pleasant London home. Some alleviation came with the sale of the film rights of *Juno* to British International Pictures. This brought them £1,000, much of which had to be spent on repairs and alterations to the house. Perhaps it was partly to help them financially, as well as realising that Eileen was missing her professional life, that Cochran invited her to audition for his next production, Noël Coward's musical *Bitter-Sweet*. After some hesitation by Coward, when he realised she was the wife of the man who had harshly criticised his early plays, Eileen was given her contract and duly joined the happy band of 'Mr Cochran's Young Ladies'. *Bitter-Sweet*, once it had settled into his Majesty's Theatre, ran until May 1931.

Preliminary arrangements for the production of *The Silver Tassie* were going ahead. Raymond Massey, the Canadian actor, was engaged to direct it, and the cast included Charles Laughton as Harry Heegan, Beatrix Lehman as Susie Monican, and Binnie Barnes as Jessie Taite. At Seán's request Barry Fitzgerald was brought from Dublin to play Sylvester Heegan. Among the soldiers in the second act was a young Welsh actor, Emlyn Williams. Cochran was intent on having Augustus John to design this act, and Eileen was sent to woo his acceptance.

5

On 19 October 1929 *The Silver Tassie* opened at the Apollo Theatre with the full glitter of a Cochran first night. Eileen was released for the night from *Bitter-Sweet* to join Cochran and his wife in their stage box. The Shaws were there, accompanying Lady Londonderry, and somewhere hidden away at the back of the theatre was Seán. The curtain rose on the second act to show John's superb set – 'the jagged and lacerated ruin of what was once a monastery', the broken life-size crucifix, the great howitzer with 'its long sinister barrel now pointing towards the front', and the strange crouching figure of a soldier 'whose clothes are covered with mud and splashed with blood'. Somewhere a small organ was playing the Introit to the

Mass. After a pause the Croucher, without moving,
[70] intoned:

> And the hand of the Lord was upon me, and carried me out in the spirit of the Lord, and set me down in the midst of a valley. And I looked and saw a great multitude that stood upon their feet, an exceeding great army. And he said unto me, Son of Man, can this exceeding great army become a valley of dried bones?

As soon as the curtain fell, Bernard Shaw was hurrying to find Seán to tell him once again that he had written 'a hell of a play'.

On the following morning Seán received a letter from Lady Gregory, telling him she was coming to London, hoping to see the play, and looking forward to visiting him in his new house, 'if you invite me – to see and make acquaintance with your wife and son'.[16] But Seán could not bring himself to meet her despite Eileen's pleading. Greatly as he loved her, the rejection of his play by the Abbey still rankled, and 'Bitterness would certainly enter into things I would say about W. B. Yeats and L. Robinson, if we were to meet, bitterness that would hurt you, and I am determined to avoid hurting you as much as possible.'[17] Again she appealed to him before she left London: 'Your letter has grieved me – perhaps I deserve it – but I do ask you to change your mind.' There was no reply. Sadly she wrote in her journal: 'We ought not to have rejected it. We should have held out against Lennox Robinson that last evening when the order to return it was given.'[18] Many years later Seán was to regret his hasty rejection of his old friend:

> So Lady Gregory went back to Ireland, without a word with him; without a last affectionate hand-

shake, for he never laid eyes on her again. This refusal was one of his silly sins. He still thinks angrily of himself when he thinks of her, or hears the name of the gracious, gallant woman. He should have listened to Eileen.[19]

The generally enthusiastic reception of the play by the London critics and the support and praise he received from his friends did much to heal the wound of the Abbey's rejection; Gabriel Fallon came from Ireland to see the play twice to find 'the play in action to be as theatrically effective and as deeply moving as I found it in the reading'.[20] The first week's receipts broke the record of the Apollo for the past three years, and there was talk of a New York production. It must have seemed to Seán and Eileen that their immediate financial problems might well be at an end. But Fate was about to strike again. During the second week of the production the Wall Street stock-market crashed, resulting in a chain reaction throughout the money markets of the world, and in Britain two and a half million unemployed. Inevitably theatres were among the first to feel the effects of the depression. Cochran was no believer in skimping his theatrical ventures, and the heavy running costs of *The Silver Tassie* made it economically unviable. After eight weeks it had to close. Prospects of a production in Dublin's Gaiety Theatre, which Fallon was endeavouring to organise, fell through as a result of adverse criticism by the Church. Father Michael Henry Gaffney, OP, wrote in the *Catholic Mind*:

> Dublin is to have the opportunity in the Autumn of drinking deep from *The Silver Tassie*. But I fancy that Dublin is a little too wise to put its lips to a cup that may possibly have been filled from a sewer. The play has been published in

> London, and is in our hands for cold inspection.
> [72] It defies analysis. It is a vigorous medley of lust and hatred and vulgarity.[21]

In New York the play opened at the Greenwich Village Theatre on 24 October 1930 and closed after forty performances.

In September 1931 Seán and Eileen were forced to sell the remainder of their lease of 19 Woronzow Road, and on McElroy's advice moved to a rented cottage in Chalfont St Giles, Buckinghamshire. 'It was the silliest move we had made; town people at heart we ought to have rented a cheaper flat in London.'[22]

5
Citizen of the World

1

The Silver Tassie marks a turning-point in O'Casey's dramatic work, as well as in the range of his vision. It heralds his final break with the naturalistic play and opens up his field of vision to include the world outside Ireland.

In *The Flying Wasp*, a collection of essays attacking the conservatism of the British stage and its urbane critics, he wrote:

> We do not want merely an excerpt from reality; it is the imaginative translation of reality, as it is seen through the eye of the poet, that we desire. The great art of the theatre is to suggest, not to tell openly; to dilate the mind by symbols, not by actual things; to express in *Lear* a world's sorrow, and in *Hamlet* the grief of humanity.[1]

At the same time he had this to say about dramatic form:

> Sculpture, architecture, literature, poetry, and the domestic arts are effectively walking about in new ways, and drama isn't going to stay quietly in her picture frame gazing coyly out at changing life around her, like a languid invalid woman looking pensively out of a window in the fourth wall.[2]

However, he was not to be bound by any single school of play-writing. The expressionist techniques he employed so effectively in the second act of *The*

Silver Tassie were only one of the instruments he was
[74] to use in his search for new forms with which to express his wider view of life. Nor was he to abandon naturalism completely. Unlike the continental expressionists, he continued to enrich his plays with that warm breath of humanity that constitutes an essential part of 'the O'Casey touch'.

His critics and many of his admirers have said that by exiling himself from Ireland and from Dublin O'Casey lost much of his fire and force. In fact he never lost touch with Dublin or his native land; but the Ireland that was emerging during the 1930s under the guidance of de Valera no longer provided the stage for the dramatic conflicts that were the background of his earlier plays. Gone were the utopian dreams of Pádraic Pearse; gone too were Larkin's dreams of a workers' republic. The new Ireland bore all the signs of a petty-bourgeois ascendancy: pietistic, parochial, commercial and conservative. Divorce was prohibited; the sale and import of contraceptives was illegal. There was censorship of films and literature to an extent that often brought ridicule on the country. Few writers of eminence, dead or alive, escaped condemnation; O'Casey was no exception. The influence of a puritanical Catholic Church was all-pervasive. Its special position as the guardian of the faith of the majority of the citizens was recognised in the 1937 constitution. In country districts the parish priest assumed the position of an autocrat, not only as the guardian of the morals of his flock but also as the preserver of social attitudes that were being rapidly discarded in the world outside. Furthermore, he was the manager of the local National School. His influence thus extended from childhood to the grave.

Writing many years later of the Ireland that was the subject of O'Casey's later plays, Seán O'Faolain had this to say:

We must finally understand that the class that thus came to power and influence was not a labouring class; the more able among them changed their nature by changing their place in life – they graduated rapidly into *petit bourgeois*, middleman, importers, small manufacturers, thus forming a new middle class to fill the vacuum formed by the departure or depression of the alien middle class. These men, naturally, had very little education and could have only a slight interest in the intellectual's fight for liberty of expression. . . . In any case, since they were rising to sudden wealth behind protective tariff walls, they had a vested interest in nationalism and even in isolationism. The upshot of it was a holy alliance between the Church, the new businessmen, and the politicians, all three nationalist–isolationist for, respectively, moral reasons, commercial reasons, and politico-patriotic reasons. The intellectuals became a depressed group. Possibly they were also affected by the atmosphere around them. When patriotism starts to cash in it is enough to sicken anyone.[3]

In this atmosphere O'Casey, with his outspoken attacks on the Church, his championship of youth and free enjoyment of sexual relations when sanctified by love, had no place. And because he was Irish in every breath, and no city so dear to his heart as Dublin, he had to attack this new Ireland with all the ridicule and invective that he had previously used to fight against British rule. This he could only do from outside the country, and by placing it in perspective with the wider world of which he was now a citizen.

This was a world in the process of a revolution so radical that today we are still unable to see or prophesy to what end it will lead. The Wall Street crash, resulting in the economic depression of the 1930s, brought unemployment and misery to millions throughout [76] America and Europe. In Britain there were nearly three million 'on the dole'. It shook the foundations of the capitalist world. It provided the breeding-ground not only for Communism but also for Fascism: for Mussolini's Blackshirts in Italy, Hitler's Brownshirts in Germany, Mosley's British Union of Fascists, General O'Duffy's Blueshirts in Ireland, Franco's Falangists in Spain. It led to the massacre of Guernica, the gas-chambers of Auschwitz and Buchenwald, to the slaughter and destruction of the Second World War with its climax in the furnace of Hiroshima and Nagasaki. There followed a post-war world swept by the 'winds of change', bringing the fall of old empires and the rise of new ones more tyrannical than the old. Social orders and beliefs that had stood for centuries were uprooted and cast aside. This was to be the background of O'Casey's tragic moralities: *Within the Gates*, *The Star Turns Red*, *Oak Leaves and Lavender*; while in his comic moralities, *Cock-a-Doodle Dandy*, *The Bishop's Bonfire* and *The Drums of Father Ned*, and in his short fantasies, *Figuro in the Night*, *The Moon Shines on Kylenamoe* and *Behind the Green Curtains* he attacked with merciless satire the social pretentions, the materialistic and politico-religious attitudes of 'de Valera's Island'.

In Ireland itself O'Casey was regarded by many as the devil's advocate. In 1930 the film of *Juno and the Paycock* was burned in the streets of Limerick. When *The Silver Tassie* was eventually presented at the Abbey in 1936 it raised such a storm of protest that the novelist and playwright Brinsley Macnamara, the only Catholic member of the directorate present at the time, took fright and denounced the production of the play he had previously sanctioned. Another storm of protest and abuse surrounded the production of *The Bishop's Bonfire* in 1955. In 1958 permission for a votive Mass to mark the opening of the second Dublin Theatre Festival was withdrawn when it was learned that O'Casey's play *The Drums of Father Ned* was to be included in the schedule of events.

The often repeated assertion that by breaking with the Abbey Seán lost the necessary workshop to shape and test his experiments is to ignore these facts. If the Abbey had harboured and encouraged the sort of plays that O'Casey wanted to write, it would have lost both its audience and its government subsidy. In England Seán was at least free to express his views without fear of oppression, even if his views found little favour with the majority of the playgoers and reading public, for he did not spare his criticisms of Britain – its philistine attitude to the arts, the vacuity of its theatre, its class structure and its politics.

2

Despite his attacks on the Church, Seán was not anti-Christian; rather he was against those so-called Christians who abused Christ's teaching and who denied the fullness of life on this earth with their doctrine of eternal damnation. Christ, he argued, was crucified again by a Church that condoned the poverty, disease and misery of the slums, piling 'the weight and wealth and power of mighty buildings on top of the grave of Jesus, driving him deeper down'.[4]

In his next play, *Within the Gates*, which he completed in 1933, the Dreamer, obviously a spokesman for the author, says: 'Offer not as incense to God the dust of your sighing, but dance to His glory and come before His presence with a song!' This vision of a God of human happiness, a God of art and dance and song, is endowed with pagan overtones. These are present not only in an almost bacchinalian form of worship, but also in the nature imagery scattered

throughout the play, and even in the play's construc-
[78] tion, as epitomised by its four acts – spring, summer, autumn and winter – and in the celebratory hymns to spring and summer. O'Casey's plea in *Within the Gates* is for the worship of God through the fullness of life on this earth, not 'through the fear of His judgement to come'. Neither established Christianity, in the character of the Bishop, nor the Atheist, who has no time for a song, can bring peace to the Young Whore, forced into prostitution by capitalist exploitation and dying of a heart disease. Nor can she find comfort from the Salvationist with his message of repentance and everlasting peace in another world, nor from the Gardener, who offers love without commitment. It is only when death approaches that she finds reconciliation with God through the Dreamer's celebration of life, urging her to turn her back on the Bishop and his calls for her repentance.

> *Dreamer (to Young Whore):* Turn your back swift on the poor, purple-button'd Dead-man, whose name is absent from the book of life. Offer not as incense to God the dust of your sighing, but dance to His glory and come before His presence with a song!
>
> *The Young Whore (with reckless defiance):* I'll go the last few steps of the way rejoicing; I'll go game, and I'll die dancing.

Yet when she collapses and the Bishop comes to her aid, her dying request is that he should guide her hand to make the sign of the cross 'that I may whisper my trust in the golden mercy of God'.

Are we, then, to presume that the Young Whore becomes a balancing factor between the two forms of religious philosophy, that of the Dreamer, with his exaltation of life and joy, and that of the Bishop, with his call for worship through 'repentance' and 'a sigh'?

The answer is equivocal. O'Casey seems to have reached a critical juncture in his attitude to religious belief; he is uncertain which road to take. If he no longer accepts religion, he has not totally rejected it. The same equivocation appears in the political philosophy of the play. As yet Seán had not fully committed himself to Communism. He had seen the failure of capitalism in the Wall Street crash and the subsequent depression, and he had also seen the failure of the Labour Party's brand of socialism in the collapse of the second Ramsay MacDonald administration. The doom-like chorus of the Down-and-Outs with its sinister drum-beats epitomises the defeatist attitude of the unemployed proletariat:

> We challenge life no more, no more with
> our dead faith and our dead hope. . . .

In contrast O'Casey provides the Dreamer's reply:

> Sorrow and pain we shall have, and struggle
> unending;
> We shall weave courage with pain, and fight
> through the struggle unending.
> Way for the strong and the swift and the
> fearless;
> Life that is weak with the terror of life let
> it die;
> Let it sink down, let it die, and pass from
> our vision for ever!

But how and where the struggle is to take place, between whom and about what, the Dreamer fails to tell. It is not until his next play, *The Star Turns Red*, that O'Casey reaches a more explicit political attitude with his final acceptance of Communism. His substitution of a vague worship of art in the place of organised religion was, as Desmond Greaves points out, not untypical of many 'gifted and artistic young

people [of the mid-1930s] whose prospects had been
[80] blighted by the slump'.[5] Some, like O'Casey, were subsequently to seek salvation in Communism, albeit temporarily.

Within the Gates was first conceived as a film, but after an abortive discussion with Alfred Hitchcock, who had made the film of *Juno and the Paycock*, Seán turned it into a play at first called *The Green Gates*, in which the Park – obviously Hyde Park – is a microcosm of Britain during the economic depression.

When he first came to London Seán was drawn to Hyde Park with its passing parade of nursemaids, chattering about their respective mistresses and drooling over their infant charges, its tramps and whores, the guardsmen walking out with their lassies, the riders in Rotten Row, and Speaker's Corner with its assortment of oddities thundering out their messages of doom and salvation. In an early interview with Beverly Nichols he is reported as saying:

> Yesterday was the happiest I've spent since I came to England. It was in Hyde Park that I spent it, and I stood there listening to the speakers. I felt almost drunk at the end of it – the characters up there are so rich in comedy. *What are your dramatists doing to neglect Hyde Park*?[6]

Gabriel Fallon, who visited the O'Caseys in London in 1929, tells a similar tale of Seán's excitement as they listened to the speakers in the park.

Within the Gates, with its use of chants, the representational naming of characters and its patterned symbolism, is O'Casey's first completely expressionist play. 'I am out to destroy the accepted naturalistic presentation of character; to get back to the poetic significance of drama,' he told a correspondent of the *New York Times*[7] when the play was presented on

Broadway in 1934. In fact Seán created a gallery of miniature character studies in the form of the Chair Attendants, the Guardsman, the Nursemaids, the Policewoman, the Man with the Stick, and so forth. These do much to relieve the stylised treatment of the main characters. But the play contains too many incidents, too many 'wild themes and wandering dialogue' to be easily digestible. Divorced from contact with the live theatre by his self-imposed exile from Ireland and by his removal from London, Seán seems to be writing for the play-reader. *Within the Gates* was published in 1933, but it was not until a year later that he could find a theatre willing to produce it. [81]

3

The 1930s were years of frustration and anxiety for the O'Caseys. Financial problems were becoming increasingly urgent, so that Eileen was forced to continue her stage work. This entailed her staying in London during the week, leaving Seán to suffer alone the boring, conventional society of Chalfont St Giles. His health was poor, owing to his chain-smoking, and at one point he was thought to have a serious heart condition. Moreover, by July 1932 he was seriously in debt. In a letter to the Inspector of Taxes Seán wrote:

> Dear Sir,
>
> I have only twenty pounds in the whole world, but I send you, as ordered, Five Pounds to keep the wolf from the door, leaving myself with Fifteen to keep myself, wife and kid, and help to promulgate the Gospel in foreign parts.
>
> I appreciate your point that my debt to the Inland Revenue is now £236 odd, but it won't be higher on account of last year's Income, for there

was none, for which I cannot thank God. With [82] your permission, I should like to make a point myself, and it is this: when we poor devils of Artists get anything, we get it all at once, and not regularly, as others do, so that we have to pay more taxes than most persons. There seems to be a core of injustice in that. . . .

I have just finished a little one-act play, which I hope to see on the Halls. . . . I hope, too, within the next three or four months, to finish my big play [*Within the Gates*] which I am sure will be anything but popular, but may, I hope, add to the honour of drama written in the English tongue. . . .[8]

In an attempt to meet his debts he sold half the amateur rights of his three Dublin plays to Samuel French for £300, against the strong advice of Bernard Shaw. It was a decision he was to regret. The 'little one-act play' mentioned in his letter to the Inspector of Taxes was a delightful and typical O'Casey farce, *A Pound on Demand*, one of a pair – the other being *The End of the Beginning* – that he wrote for Arthur Sinclair, who was comtemplating a tour of the music-halls. In the event neither was produced by him. (*A Pound on Demand* was eventually produced at the Q Theatre, Richmond, on 16 October 1934; *The End of the Beginning* had to wait until 8 February 1937 for its first performance, when it was put on at the Abbey Theatre.)

Ill fortune seemed to have cast a dark cloud over his London success as a playwright. *Within the Gates* was reluctantly turned down by Cochran, who was himself experiencing financial difficulties. In a letter to Seán he wrote: 'You can't go on writing fine things, Seán, unless they bring some material reward. I suppose you are tired of people advising you to get back to the method of "Juno". I wish you would.' To which Seán replied: 'Your advice to go back to the genius of "Juno" might be good for me, but bad for my conception of the drama.'[9]

The anger and indignation that he felt over the rejection of *The Silver Tassie* still lingered. Yeats had, he believed, dealt a cruel blow at his career as a playwright, and now he had to start all over again. A note of the 'savage indignation' that he shared with Swift, that was to create many enemies and lose him many friends, began to enter his published articles and letters to the press. In October 1932 he refused membership of Yeats's Irish Academy of Letters, claiming that 'The censorship of dull authority embattled in this Irish Academy of Letters will be much more dangerous to the Irish authors than the *Domine dirige nos* censorship exercised by the State and Church.'[10] 'Oh! dear Seán, don't be too belligerent!' wrote Charlotte Shaw. 'God be my judge', he replied, 'that I hate fighting. If I be damned for anything, I shall be damned for keeping the two-edged sword of thought in its scabbard when it should be searching the bowels of knaves and fools.'[11] When *Within the Gates* eventually opened in London under the direction of Norman MacDermot at the Royalty Theatre, his two-edged sword was wielded with a vengeance.

The play opened on 7 February 1934. Seán attended the rehearsals, he and Eileen having been lent a flat in St James's Square by Lady Astor. It was an unhappy experience. There was constant friction between him and MacDermot over the production, and he also quarrelled with Herbert Hughes, who adapted and composed the music, over the division of royalties. Despite a fine cast, including Basil Bartlett as the Dreamer, Douglas Jefferies as the Bishop, and Marjorie Mars as the Young Whore, the play only ran for twenty-eight performances. The reviews were generally unfavourable, except for one in *The Times* in which

Charles Morgan wrote: 'Mr O'Casey's fierce play is
[84] that very rare thing – a modern morality play that is not a pamphlet but a work of art. . . . He is opening up a new country of the imagination from which, by its rigid photography, the fashionable theatre has hitherto been shut out.' James Agate in the *Sunday Times*, however, called the play 'pretentious rubbish', adding that 'Having spoken of O'Casey as the greatest living dramatist but one . . . we will cross out "rubbish" and leave the word "pretentious".' In the *Daily Express* Gordon Beckles challenged O'Casey 'to tell the world what the play is really about'. Both were to receive fierce thrusts from his sword.

Beckles was quickly dispatched. 'Gordon Beckles challenges me to tell him what the play really means. My mission in life is not to give Gordon Beckles a higher mind than he has, for I am not a worker of miracles.'[12] Agate was another matter. Seán seems to have taken a dislike to him ever since he first met him in the Garrick Club. 'Seán wouldn't grapple this fellow to him with any hook of steel . . . a small man in spite of his bulkiness; a small inhabitant of a smaller world.'[13] He answered Agate's criticism in one of the longest letters ever printed in the *Sunday Times*, but his full indignation against this leading critic was reserved for the future publication of *The Flying Wasp* in 1937.

Generous praise was, however, forthcoming to offset the barbs of his English critics. From New York George Jean Nathan, to whom he had sent a copy of the published play, wrote: 'I want to tell you in all heartfelt critical sincerity that it is one of the most beautiful plays I have read for a long, long time.'[14] Eugene O'Neill was also impressed, telling Seán: 'It is a splendid piece of work. My enthusiastic congratulations to you. I was especially moved – and greatly envious I confess! by its rare and sensitive poetical beauty. I wish to God I could write like that!'[15] Nathan, with the collaboration of the literary and dramatic agent Richard J. Madden, set to work to find a suitable management to present the play in New York. On 14 March O'Casey signed a contract with George Bushar Markle and John Tuerk for a production due to open in the autumn. Tickets were sent for his passage to New York to help with the rehearsals. As Eileen was pregnant, she was unable to accompany him, and the O'Caseys decided to leave Chalfont St Giles and take a London flat, 49 Overstrand Mansions, overlooking Battersea Park. On 13 September 1934 Seán sailed from Southampton, having spent a week with Lord and Lady Londonderry at Mount Stewart, their home in Northern Ireland. He had £15 in his pocket and, by arrangement with the Londonderrys, a guarantee of £200 at the bank. In addition to his customary cloth cap, he was wearing a new suit provided by Lady Astor. Seán the proletarian was never averse to accepting the gifts and hospitality of the aristocracy. This is no criticism of his integrity, for he never concealed his political opinions from them, nor muted his criticism. It is a tribute both to Seán and to his aristocratic friends that each respected the other's sincerity. Among those friends his warmest affection was reserved for Lady Gregory. When she died in 1932 he wrote:

> I loved her and I think she was fond of me – why God only knows. Our friendship affinity was an odd one; she an aristocrat and I a proletarian Communist. Yet we understood each other well. . . . It was (and still is) a bitter memory within me that the difference between the Directorate and me over *The Silver Tassie* separated us for ever.[16]

On 19 September the *Majestic* docked in New York. Seán was practically penniless. As a first-class passenger he was obliged to be generous beyond his [86] means, and his modest £15 had been swallowed up in the customary tips. He was also highly apprehensive of what sort of reception he would receive. But there on the quayside were Dick Madden and George Nathan, holding out hands of welcome and guiding him through the waiting reporters and photographers with their barrage of questions and magnesium flashlights. Here was not just another celebrity, but a genuine curiosity, good for a column or two in the city's bulky newspapers – the slum playwright from the Emerald Isle, complete with genuine brogue, tweed suit, and cloth cap perched jauntily over one eye; the man whose plays caused riots and were hailed as works of a genius. Even his scanty luggage attracted attention: it consisted of a single small suitcase which, according to Eugene O'Neill's biographers, contained – apart from the clothes he stood up in – an extra set of underwear, a single shirt, a pair of socks and a sweater.[17]

> I have been surrounded with interviewers [he wrote to Lady Londonderry] who have asked me all the things that happened to me since I gave my first cry coming into this world. The people are very kind and hospitable, placing all New York at my feet; but I have selected cautiously, and am living as quietly as I would were I lounging about London – except for rehearsals which take up a lot of my time.[18]

It was not long before he was caught up in the hectic mill-race of New York's life, guided by Dick Madden and that 'Prince of Dramatic Critics and Prince among men', George Nathan. Those favoured with the warmth of his friendship, his wit, hospitality and sophistication could wish no better guide to the New York theatre, or to its best food and wine, whether at his table in the Stork Club or in any other of his favourite haunts where good company and feminine charm surrounded him and the only mortal sin was to bore. Seán was also befriended, and the cause of his play championed, by Brooks Atkinson of the *New York Times.* Among his new friends were Eugene O'Neill, Sinclair Lewis and Elmer Rice.

New York was a stimulating experience. The bustling life of the city with its giant skyscrapers reaching up to a brilliant blue sky was the symbol of a new world. Looking back many years later to his visit, he recalled the emotions he experienced in looking up at the Rockefeller Center: 'No cathedral equalled this building of New York in its height, its cool beauty, its significance for the present world – not even Wren's St Paul's or Angelo's St Peter's. It was the new replacing the old; the old that had lost it's meaning and use.'[19]

Within the Gates opened at the National Theatre on 22 October, directed by Melvyn Douglas and with a cast that included Bramwell Fletcher as the Dreamer, Moffat Johnson as the Bishop, and Lilian Gish, whose friendship he cherished, as the Young Whore. The reviews were divided between high praise and cool comment, but none were dismissive. Once the play had opened, Seán was pressed to address clubs and societies – something he particularly abhorred. 'I don't lecture, and anything I should say would be in the nature of an informal talk,'[20] he wrote to Horace Reynolds who invited him to talk on Elizabethan drama to the Harvard Poetry Society. But the thing that frightened and harassed him most were the women's clubs.

> It was a flutter of the heart to have to say yes, for the sake of the play, to an invitation to come and speak to one of the gigantic gatherings. He felt as Moses did when asked by God to go to Egypt

and speak on behalf of the chosen people. But
[88] go he had to, for these clubs bought bunches of tickets for a play, and were very powerful.[21]

The play prospered, running for 102 nights; thereafter a tour of thirteen cities was arranged. Seán left New York on 12 December full of hope: it seemed certain that the royalties from the tour would provide security for Eileen and the growing O'Casey family for at least another year.

4

On 23 December he landed in Liverpool to learn that *Windfalls*, published in October and containing the story 'I Wanna Woman', had been banned in Ireland by the newly established Censorship of Publications Board. On 15 January 1935 came another blow. In Boston Mayor Frederick W. Mansfield banned *Within the Gates* on grounds of immorality and blasphemy, pressurised to do so by the Rev. Russell M. Sullivan, SJ, head of the League of Decency, and Bishop Charles W. Burns of the Wesleyan Church. 'The coo of the Wesleyan pigeon was aligned with the croak of the Jesuit raven.'[22] Father Sullivan was supported by the Rev. Terence Connelly, SJ, drama critic of the magazine *America*, who declared: 'In spots it is unspeakable filth, drenched with sex and written to point out the futility of religion.'[23] The Wesleyan bishop, who had neither read nor seen the play, stated that he was 'told' that his preachers had voted to protest against it because of what they had been 'told' by Father Sullivan.

The action of the 'Puritan Fathers' did not go unchallenged. A storm of protest was raised by students at Harvard and by many others, but the damage was done. The banning of the play in Boston led to the cancellation of the tour; and, although the management revived the play in New York, where it ran for a further forty performances, gone were Seán's hopes of security for Eileen and the children – for, to add to the irony of the situation, on the same day that the play was banned the O'Caseys' second son, Niall, was born. Seven years earlier the news of the Abbey's rejection of *The Silver Tassie* had reached Seán on the day his first son came into the world.

Injustice, be it to others or himself, was a fuse that never failed to set off the explosions of 'savage indignation' that lay dormant in Seán's nature: blasts that were often unjust and unworthy of his genius. Even when justified, his criticisms were, more often than not, more damaging to himself than to those he attacked.

In February 1935 he accepted an invitation from Kingsley Martin, editor of the *New Statesman*, to review the published book of Ronald Gow's and Walter Greenwood's stage adaptation of the latter's novel, *Love on the Dole*. His review of the play, which he had not seen, was both abusive and unwise. 'There isn't a character in it worth a curse, and there isn't a thought in it worth remembering.'[24] Critics had compared the play, which proved highly successful, to *Juno and the Paycock*. Inevitably Seán's attack could be mistaken for jealously. Such at any rate was suggested in a letter of protest from Ethel Mannin – one of the many received by the *New Statesman*.

A few days after this attack he refused to review George Orwell's novel, *A Clergyman's Daughter*. His letter to the publishers[25] was scarcely likely to endear him to the author, who in due course delivered a scathing review of *Drums Under the Window*, the third volume of O'Casey's autobiography.

In *Time and Tide*, to whose column 'Notes on the Way' he was a guest contributor, he widened his attack

on *Love on the Dole* to include the 'kid-glove' treat-
[90] ment given by English critics in their reviews of 'worthless plays'. However, this controversy had one happy aspect in that it brought about a reconciliation between himself and Yeats. Yeats, who was ill at the time, received a sympathetic letter from O'Casey 'which gave me great pleasure'. He reciprocated the friendly gesture by writing to Ethel Mannin reproving her for her attack on Seán. As a result, Yeats and Seán dined together in London, and it was agreed that the Abbey should now present *The Silver Tassie*.

The play was presented at the Abbey on 12 August 1935, directed by Arthur Shields and with F. J. McCormick in the part of Harry Heegan. The reactions of the Irish critics and clergy were predictable: it was condemned even before it opened as 'blasphemous', 'brutally offensive', 'a vigorous medley of lust, and hatred and vulgarity'. The Abbey director, Brinsley Macnamara, in a letter to the *Irish Independent*, wrote: 'I did not see the play until the second night of its production and my immediate feelings were that an outrage had been committed.' He then proceeded to castigate the Abbey audiences for their 'wholly uncritical and, I might say, almost insane admiration for the vulgar and worthless plays of Mr O'Casey'.[26] The President of the Gaelic League, Father P. T. McGinley, issued a public statement in which he condemned the play – naturally he had not seen it – and demanded that the Abbey be abolished. From now until the end of his life Seán was destined to be at loggerheads with the Irish Catholic Church, never missing an opportunity to attack what he considered to be its puritanical and hypocritical attitudes. There was, however, one Catholic writer who supported him, the actor Robert Speaight, who wrote in the *Catholic Herald*:

> The play is an outcry from a passionate and embittered mind. But it is much nearer to Christianity, [91] because it is nearer to life, than the complaisant criticism levelled against it. The soul of the bourgeoisie has betrayed itself. This surely is the essence of the bourgeois mind – that it cannot look tragedy in the face: for O'Casey has seen into the heart of the horror of war and wrenched out its dreadful secret; that the co-heirs of Christ destroy one another in the sight of the son of man.[27]

In September Seán and Eileen paid a private visit to Dublin in order to settle questions arising out of the death of Eileen's grandfather, who had died intestate. Happily Seán was able to cement his reconciliation with Yeats over a game of croquet – 'A game in which Yeats played like a champion. The only game of croquet Seán had ever played; the only one he would ever play, played with the poet Yeats.'[28] This was to be Seán's last visit to his native city, and his last meeting with Yeats.

The year 1935, however, brought some compensation to lighten the bitterness he felt over the cancellation of the American tour of *Within the Gates*. The sale of the film rights of *The Plough and the Stars* to RKO was a boon to his ailing finances. Directed by John Ford, the film was released in March 1937. The cast included Barry Fitzgerald as Fluther Good, Barbara Stanwyck as Nora, and Preston Foster as Jack Clitheroe. Several of the leading Abbey players also took part. As a film it was a considerable improvement on Hitchcock's *Juno and the Paycock*.

But this break in the dark clouds of his fortunes did not deter him from his self-appointed role of castigating the theatre of his time – and not only the theatre. Invited to address the Shirley Society at St Catherine's College, Cambridge, in January 1936,

he delivered a scathing denunciation of English poli-
[92] tics, sport, smugness and conventional attitudes in a speech which he entitled 'The Holy Ghost Leaves England'. In *Time and Tide* he attacked Noël Coward in an article entitled 'Coward Codology'.[29] Accused by James Agate in the *Sunday Times* of lack of generosity, he retaliated with an article, 'Swat That Wasp', in which he reminded the critic of his own onslaught on those intellectuals who decried Coward, adding: 'I am a flying wasp that Mr Agate will never be able to kill.'[30]

The Flying Wasp, the title of which was derived from Agate's article and Seán's reply, was published in March 1937. It was the vehicle for a series of onslaughts – many reprinted from previous essays – against the British stage; its writers – Coward, Philpotts, Lonsdale, Nicholls; its critics – Agate, Ivor Brown, Edward Shanks; its neglect of Shakespeare; its failure to establish a national theatre; and its out-of-date attachment to the proscenium stage. Harold Macmillan, as his publisher, urged him to modify the 'combative' tone of his criticisms. In reply Seán wrote: 'I know these sayings will not make it easier for me, and I love ease; but not enough to change what I believe to be the truth into politeness and nicety of speech and manner.'[31] Yet amidst the fire and smoke of his critical blasts a very different Seán O'Casey was writing the moving, tragic, and humorous story of John Casside and his heroic mother in a series of sketches that were to become the first – and arguably most brilliant – of the six volumes of his autobiography.

6
The Red Star and the Cross

1

The 1930s saw the rapid growth of Fascism and Communism in nearly all countries of the western world. In 1936 the physical clash between them in the Spanish Civil War was a catalyst that determined the allegiance of many intellectuals who previously had found no certain anchor for their ideals or who had skirted on the fringes of Marxist principles. Seán maintained he had been a Communist from the time he began his dramatic career. 'I never lost my Communism, it merely changed by growing deeper within me,' he wrote many years later to Saros Cowasjee.[1] Nevertheless, it was not until the mid-1930s that he began to profess his Communist faith publicly. In November 1935 he confessed to Lady Astor that there was 'something in Communism', to which she replied: 'I would like to take you to Russia – I don't know anybody who would be less fitted to live under an autocracy than you, unless it is myself!'[2]

It seems that for Seán as for others 1936 was the crucial year that finally induced him to abandon the artistic elitism that governed his outlook at the time when he was writing *Within the Gates.* The point has been well made by Desmond Greaves in his book, *Seán O'Casey: Politics and Art*, drawing attention to the considerable increase in O'Casey's references to Communism and the USSR in letters and articles from 1936 onwards.[3] Seán was never a card-carrying member of the British Communist Party, though he

was a frequent contributor to the *Daily Worker*, and
[94] from 1940 to 1952 a member of its editorial board; but his allegiance to its creed was confirmed in a letter written to Horace Reynolds of Yale University on 5 January 1937: 'As for me, once a Communist, always a Communist.'[4] In October 1938 he wrote the first of his articles for the Moscow journal *International Literature*: 'Then the thing for England to do (even for her own selfish sake) is to bring to power in England a Party, that so far from being afraid of the USSR, will seek in every possible way to gain her support. . . . A union with her brings the certainty of peace; and in peace alone, can the Arts and Sciences blossom.'[5] Seán's enthusiasm for the cause was only matched by his political naïvety. From now on, as if to share his faith with his friends, he assured such unlikely candidates as Harold Macmillan and George Jean Nathan that they too were good Communists.

As a Communist he was at pains to declare himself an atheist. But the legacy of his family background and his own religious experience was not easily shaken off. Throughout his later works O'Casey was struggling to find a way of uniting Christianity and Communism – the Star of Bethlehem with the Red Star. 'Like Shaw I am an Atheist, and I thank God for it,' he declared in a letter to the *Irish Times* in August 1938.[6] Writing to Gabriel Fallon in March 1937, he asked:

> I wonder why do so many priests say that Communism emphatically denies the existence of God, and that a Communist must necessarily be an Atheist? If they would read the Communist Manifesto – our Creed – they'd find there no denial of God's existence. Communists are no more concerned with this matter than are Conservatives, except that Conservatives . . . make use of God for peculiar & personal purposes, and that, if God

exists, is a terrible thing to do. . . . Over here there's a row on in Parliament about a Communist Poster that has superimposed a hammer and sickle on the Cross. This seems funny to me, for what holier symbols – in a very high earthly sense – have we than the sickle & the hammer? And if I may say so, from what I have often read about Christ, I'd go bail He often used a hammer, & probably knew, & knows how to use it well; & possibly, He knew something about a sickle, too, for we're told in Revelations that "And I looked, & behold a white cloud, and upon the cloud one sat like unto the Son of man, having on His head a golden crown, and in His hand a sharp Sickle." So you see . . .[7]

Like Shaw's Black Girl, he was in search of God,[8] but his vision was dimmed by his blind faith in Communism as Christ's kingdom on earth and by his stubborn refusal to accept the facts of Soviet imperialism and oppression. When he came to defining Communism 'he seldom mentioned Marx or Lenin. . . . He was more likely to quote from Christ and Shaw, Shelley and Keats, Blake and Burns, Emerson and Whitman, Ruskin and Morris.'[9] 'Christ was a great Communist,'[10] he told David Krause. Harold Macmillan in his autobiography, *Winds of Change*, wrote: 'Although he claimed to be a communist and, I think, an atheist, his was a truly Christian nature: one of the kindest and most genuine men I have known.'[11]

2

Up to now the background of O'Casey's major plays, with the possible exception of *Within the Gates*, had been concerned with the momentous events he had witnessed or in which, in one way or another, he had been personally involved. The rise of Fascism in Italy,

Spain and Germany, culminating with its clash with
[96] Communism in the Spanish Civil War, inevitably presented a powerful challenge to his dramatic muse. But, unlike the backgrounds of his previous plays, these events were outside his personal experience; for, although Mosley's Blackshirts in Britain and O'Duffy's Blueshirts in Ireland were active, they were but pale reflections of their continental originals. As a result, Seán chose to treat his next play, *The Star Turns Red*, as an allegorical morality, again making use of expressionist techniques and also some of the characteristics of the medieval morality plays. For instance, the names of some of his characters are those that one might expect to find in such plays as *Everyman* and the interludes of the early sixteenth century, derived in this case from Gaelic words: thus, as Desmond Greaves points out,[12] Sheasker is derived from the Gaelic *seascair* (well-heeled), Brallain from *breall* (a blot or mistake), Caheer from *cáchfair* (every defect). (O'Casey's continuing use of this type of obscure nomenclature in subsequent plays was to become a somewhat tiresome mannerism.) In keeping with the abstract nature of his treatment of the play, he placed the action in an anonymous city on Christmas Eve, 'Tomorrow or the Next Day'. The clash between Fascism and Communism takes place in the context of a strike situation, not unlike the 1913 Dublin lockout, with its powerful instigator, clearly based on Jim Larkin, here presented as Comrade Chief Red Jim. Obsessed as he was in his later plays with what he considered to be an unholy alliance between the Church and capitalist interests, and its oppressive dominion over the morals and expression of youth, Seán allies the priests of the Christian Front, led by the monstrous Purple Priest,* with his saffron-shirted storm-troopers.

* O'Casey changed the name of this character from the Red Priest in the published version of the play to the Purple Priest in the stage version.

At the same time – perhaps to appease his religious conscience – he created the well-meaning but helpless Brown Priest as the workers' friend. Above all shines the silver star of Bethlehem, which, as the play ends, turns red to the strains of the Internationale, prophesying the eventual victory of the proletariat over the forces of Fascism and the power of the priesthood, and symbolising O'Casey's attempts to equate Christianity with Communism.

Distractions of one kind or another made progress on the writing of the play slow. During the same period Seán was engaged in putting together, as well as adding to, a number of articles on his early childhood that he had contributed to various American journals. These he proposed to publish in book form. In February 1938 he wrote to Macmillans: 'I have a few things in hand (doing something with a play, and a few fantastic pages of biography), but they haven't reached the stage yet that would interest a publisher.'[13] In order to give these autobiographical sketches a novel-like form he decided to distance himself from them by writing in the third person, thus giving himself greater liberty to elaborate or invent as he chose. At first he seems to have little intention of writing more than one book 'containing stories about what I saw and heard, and felt during the first eleven years of my life'. The work, however, assumed its own momentum, eventually occupying in its six volumes a considerable amount of his working time during the next sixteen years. There were, too, other less worthwhile distractions delaying the progress of his new play. In March 1938 he plunged headlong into battle with Malcolm Muggeridge over the latter's condemnation in the *Daily Telegraph* of the Moscow treason trials.[14] From March to June letters and articles flew backwards and forwards in a variety of papers and journals. Hardly had this

finished when he was wielding his 'two-edged sword'
[98] in the columns of the *Irish Times* over a question about his attitude to Christianity that had been raised by Maurice Leahy during the 1938 Abbey Theatre Festival.[15]

Following these transient battles, the reader can only be saddened by the wasted talents of a writer who could rise to such heights of imaginative satire as 'The Castle Ball',[16] 'The Protestant Reformation',[17] or that brilliantly humorous confrontation on the top of Nelson's Pillar between the statue of Nelson and that of St Patrick – the latter having flown over from the Pro-Cathedral on the end of a rainbow powered by a couple of cherubs in order to inspect the riotous scene in O'Connell Street, where 'this Jim Larkin is tumbling my flock into turmoil again, snapping away from their grand lifelong chance of working an exceeding weight of glory from their hunger, wretchedness, and want'.[18]

Forced to live on the proceeds of Seán's articles and reviews in British and American journals, the O'Caseys again found themselves in straitened circumstances. Living in London was becoming increasingly expensive, and as the horizon began to darken with the threat of war, London was clearly no place to bring up a young family. An invitation to settle in America came from Seán's friend Lilian Gish. She had found a rich friend willing to pay the passage money; Maxwell Anderson was anxious to provide the family with accommodation; and all arrangements would be made for the children's education.

> I and Eileen have our own views on Education of our two boys [he wrote to Shaw], and although I have great faith in the youth and vitality of the people of America, I'm afraid I'm a little too far

spent to make a new life for myself and family outside of this poor, timid, half-dead country – with a keen eye on the possibility of Ireland.[19]

Shaw too had his views on education; although both he and Seán were ardent supporters of equal education for all, they had no difficulty in agreeing that Breon and Niall should be educated privately at Dartington Hall, a multi-cultural complex in Devonshire, comprising progressive junior and senior schools as well as drama, ballet, music, folk crafts and agricultural centres. Since the O'Caseys were unwilling to send their sons as boarders, they decided to leave their London flat, the lease of which had a further year to run, and establish themselves in Devon.

In the early autumn of 1938 they left London, having, as they thought, obtained their landlord's agreement to take over the remainder of the lease. After spending an uncomfortable period searching for a house the O'Caseys settled on 'an old Victorian house named Tingrith in Station Road, Totnes. It had large rooms, a garden in front and at the back, a garage, and an ample unused stable and loft; the rent, only eighty-five pounds a year, was extremely low compared with London costs.'[20]

The move, with all its attendant disruptions and anxieties, made further delays in Seán's progress on the play, while at the same time he was coping with the proofs of his autobiographical work, *I Knock at the Door*. Until he was established in his own study, with his table, chairs, bookcases and desk conforming as closely as possible to the pattern of his Mountjoy Square room, Seán was quite incapable of settling down to work. 'Throughout our life together he seemed to have this compulsive urge [to write] at the most awkward times imaginable.' Eileen O'Casey recalls. 'Christmas, say, or Easter, or any Bank Holiday, would certainly kindle in Seán an absolute fever to write. A move had the same effect; there was no doubt that he must be established quickly. . . . Immediately he was in, he started to write while the rest of the house was in turmoil around him.'[21]

By the beginning of February Seán had completed *The Star Turns Red* and a copy was dispatched to Nathan.

> I hope you'll see something in it. As well as being something of a confession of faith, it is, I think, a play; and possibly the best of its kind which has been written – which isn't saying a lot. There are anyhow good lines in it.[22]

But Nathan was for once critical. 'Incontrovertibly poor . . . the feeblest play O'Casey has written,' he wrote in *News Week* (29 January 1940). 'Communism, one fears, has now adversely affected Seán O'Casey as a dramatic artist, as a perusal of his latest play, *The Star Turns Red*, disturbingly hints.'[23] Even his first and devoted biographer, David Krause, has little to say in the play's favour:

> *The Star Turns Red* is an angry and humourless parable lacking in those characteristic qualities of ironic compassion and satiric comedy which distinguish not only the early tragi-comedies but *The Silver Tassie* and *Within the Gates*. An O'Casey play without the saving grace of laughter is a play without the O'Casey genius.[24]

It is true that in print the play has the appearance of a naïve political tract, an extended series of Communist slogans, with its melodramatic and totally biased conflict between the cardboard morality figures of Communist 'goodies' and Fascist 'baddies'. But however crude his political dialectics, and despite the lack of the 'saving grace of laughter', O'Casey's theatrical instinct did not desert him, for the play contains two vital elements of theatre that Aristotle called for – spectacle and poetic speech. But clearly these qualities could not be tested on the stage in 1939 when public opinion was seething with anger and anxiety over the Soviet Union's pact with Hitler's Germany. But when it was presented in the little left-wing Unity Theatre in London on 12 March 1940, under the direction of John Allen and two teams of amateur players performing on alternate nights, the ultra-conservative James Agate wrote in the *Sunday Times* (17 March):

> Mr O'Casey's play is a masterpiece. . . . I find the piece to be a *magnum opus* of compassion *and* a revolutionary work. I see in it a flame of propaganda tempered to a condition of dramatic art as an Elizabethan understood that art. . . . Now, at last, Mr O'Casey has achieved that towards which in *The Silver Tassie* and *Within the Gates* he was feeling his way.

It was not until 1978 that the play received a major production in the English-speaking world. On 27 January of that year it was produced in the Abbey under Tomás Mac Anna's direction. John Finegan in the *Evening Herald* voiced the reaction of the majority of the critics when he wrote: '*The Star Turns Red* emerged, to the astonishment of the critics, as one of the best of O'Casey's plays written in exile.'

3

Seán's anxiety to be settled in his new home in order to continue his work was soon frustrated by events. Six months after their departure from their London flat the O'Caseys received a letter from the agents demanding a year's rent in lieu of written notice.

Infuriated by this apparent injustice, Seán set aside
[102] his work to fight the case. Counsel was engaged, and he spent long hours 'wasting himself on reams of explanation and argument to prove we were in the right'.[25] However, the law and moral justice are not synonymous, and the case cost them £300 which they could ill afford. At the time Eileen was expecting her third child. Shivaun was born on 28 September, but before that date the old way of life in Europe and beyond it was to come to an end.

At eleven o'clock on the morning of Sunday 3 September the Prime Minister, Neville Chamberlain, announced over the radio that Britain was at war. Within a few minutes the wail of air-raid sirens sounded over the coasts of England. From London and the great cities came the pathetic stream of child refugees to seek shelter from the bombs in the countryside.

> Silently they came, for no fife shrilled a tune, no drum beat out the step; along in columns of companies, teachers beside them to see them safely deposited; no sound save the simple patter of their feet along the hardened road, many carrying millboard suitcases, some bearing parcels who couldn't afford more, armed with a day's ration of biscuit, tin of condensed milk, bar of chocolate and an apple. Gas-masks slung round each slender shoulder. The musk had gone from the rose. Gas-masks among the apple-trees. A new fruit growing on the human body. A growth, a tumour, a welt.[26]

Three of these sad little persons, aged between ten and four, were billeted on the O'Caseys. Eileen had to set to work to remove the nits from their hair; in addition to looking after the refugees, she was also minding the infant Shivaun, gaining her certificate in first-aid and learning how to deal with incendiary bombs. But no bombs came. In London the theatres

were closed, street lights went out, and the headlamps of cars and buses were reduced to a pin-prick of light. [103]
In the homes, factories and shops, in hospitals, military camps, and airports blackout blinds allowed no chink of light to guide the enemy planes.

> Sometimes, when all the darkness was there, Seán, armed with a walking-stick, went out by the garden gate, and tapped a way along the path beside the Plymouth road, looking forward, looking back, but seeing nothing. There were houses all round but they remained invisible and silent; hushed and waiting. There were people here, there, but they were not seen, and rarely heard in the darkness that pressed against the breast, the back, and down on the head oppressively, so silent that even the cocks seemed to have forgotten to crow.[27]

In the dark silence Britain waited beside radio sets, while the guns of the Maginot and Siegfried Lines faced each other. But no bombs fell; no gas-masks were taken out of their flimsy containers to stifle the wearer; no deadly fumes of mustard gas floated down from enemy planes. Meanwhile the armies of Soviet Russia swept down through the snows of Murmansk upon independent and neutral Finland and seized one-half of Poland. 'People make the mistake of thinking that Communists are idealists. On the contrary, we are realists,' Seán explained in a letter to Dick Madden in October. 'And Russia, anyway, has taken only what is, or was, her own – part of Ukraine and Byelo-Russia.'[28] He was to have a lot of explaining to do in the coming months.

Almost without exception, O'Casey seemed to be destined to give birth to his plays at times when they were most likely to provoke public anger and deny him fair and unbiased criticism. We have seen how his early Dublin plays came into the world when the newly born Free State was at its most sensitive to [104] criticism; how the birth of *Within the Gates*, with its unwelcome reminder of Britain's failure to cope with its massive unemployment problem, coincided with the very real fear of revolution that followed in the wake of the general strike and the Wall Street crash; how *The Star Turns Red* appeared when the popularity of the Soviet Union and Communism had reached an all-time low. In February 1940 the Macmillan Company of New York declined to publish it: 'Not only do I feel the publication of the play in America at the present time would do you immeasurable damage, but by the same token it would damage us too,' wrote the president of the company.[29] Now, in November 1940, the publication of *Purple Dust*, with its lively satirical comment on the English character and its foibles, was to add to O'Casey's unpopularity in Britain. The bombing of targets in British cities embarked upon in 1939 by the IRA, culminating in the death of five persons and seventy-five injured, made playgoers particularly sensitive to criticism, however light-hearted, from Irishmen resident in Britain. Nor did the international situation encourage a mood of humour and tolerance, for in June 1940 the dark silence was shattered and the phoney war came to an end. Germany's Panzer divisions swept through Holland and Belgium, turning the flank of the Maginot Line and pressing onwards to Paris, and France capitulated. The remnants of the British forces, pounded by the *Luftwaffe*, waited on the beaches of Dunkirk for the little ships to carry them home.

Britain stood alone, almost defenceless, awaiting invasion, its cities burning as the bombs fell and the rubble of its buildings covering both the living and the dead. In the spring of 1941 the entire centre of Plymouth – fifteen miles from the town of Totnes – was destroyed. The O'Caseys crouched in their tiny, damp cellar as the German planes roared overhead.

As the U-boats took their deadly toll of the Atlantic convoys popular anger turned against neutral Ireland. By some it was believed that the submarines threatening to cut Britain's lifeline with America were being fuelled and sheltered in the bays and inlets of the west of Ireland. Many bitterly resented the refusal of de Valera's government to allow the British Navy the use of the 'Treaty ports' in the south and west that had been handed back to Éire less than two years before the war.

As an Irishman living in England Seán was critical of Britain's war effort. 'Our first aim', he wrote 'ought to be an immediate peace, bringing a sudden and unprovided end to the pitiful struggle now going on for what is called the destruction of Hitlerism.'[30] He was also moved to defend Ireland's neutrality in emotive terms: 'I can see no reason on God's earth, or man's earth, why Irish bodies should mingle with the mangled squirming mass wriggling in pain, here and in Germany.'[31] He was to change his mind when in July 1941 the German armies were launched against the Soviet Union. But until Hitler made this fatal error, which cost Germany its eventual defeat, Seán, hampered by his unswerving loyalty to Communist Russia, felt unable to give the British war effort his wholehearted support.

It was during this tense period (June 1940 to July 1941), when Britain stood on the brink of the greatest disaster in her history, that Seán's 'wayward comedy', *Purple Dust*, was published.

The plot concerned the frustrating and outwitting of two crassly stupid English businessmen by their Irish employees. Basil Stoke and Cyril Poges, the one a self-made war profiteer, the other a university intellectual with pretentions to an aristocratic descent, have conveniently removed themselves from war-torn England to live a back-to-nature existence in [106] the Irish countryside, acquiring for this purpose a decaying Tudor mansion in which they propose to live with two lively Irish girls. A team of local workmen, whose foreman is the handsome young Communist Jack O'Killigain, recently returned from fighting the Fascists in Spain, manage to reduce the whole house to a shambles. Eventually O'Killigain and his colleague, Philib O'Dempsey, elope with the girls, leaving the two capitalists to their allegorical fate as the rising river sweeps away the 'purple dust' of their decaying mansion.

At any other time this satirical romp, with its songs and splendidly farcical situations, could hardly be expected to raise a ripple of serious resentment; but British audiences in 1940 were in no mood to be teased by O'Casey, even if he had some fierce things to say about contemporary Ireland as well. Lines such as 'In a generation or so the English empire with be remembered as a half-forgotten nursery rhyme', however prophetic, did not encourage commercial managements to risk offending their wartime audiences. Like *The Star Turns Red*, the play was first presented in Britain by an amateur company; it was put on at the People's Theatre, Newcastle-on-Tyne, in December 1943.

Clearly Seán had conceived *Purple Dust* as a harmless skit on the follies 'of those who see beauty in old things just because they are old . . . and how dismal a thing it is to try to live beside things and traditions that have passed away for ever'.[32] But doubts about what he had written seem to be present when, in forwarding the play to Nathan in New York, he wrote: 'I think it is, in some ways, an odd play. . . . At first it was just a skit on the country, but it changed a little into, maybe, a kind of allegorical form.'[33] In a letter to Gabriel Fallon he showed that he was fully aware that he had written something different from his original conception:

> The play was begun and well on its way without a thought of symbolism, being named simply "A Stay in the Country". I, being tired of controversy about my plays, determined to write at least one that couldn't cause any comment, and that would go on and be seen through bursts of laughter; and incidentally bring me in a few quid badly needed. . . . The play simply grew out of what I first thought, and only when it was finished in its rough form (which means three-quarters done) did I see its implications. I'm afraid I've builded better than I knew.'[34]

However, Nathan liked the play, and Dick Madden was able to write that Eddie Dowling, the New York impresario and actor, was proposing to acquire it for production on Broadway in December. Meanwhile a revival of *Juno* was bringing some welcome dollars to the ever-present needs of the O'Casey household.

But as so often happened in Seán's life, it was when Fate seemed to smile upon him that its bitterest blows were delivered. Macmillan's publishing house in New York, to whom he had offered the play, contrary to his previous practice of offering his works to the London office first, decided against publication on the grounds that they were unwilling to offend the strong pro-British sentiment of the time. There was bad news also about the production, which was first postponed and then finally abandoned by the American management. It was not until 1956 that the play was presented in New York, when it ran for four months, a record for an O'Casey play, at the off-Broadway Cherry Tree Theatre. It proved one of the most popular productions when presented by the Berliner Ensemble at the Deutsches Teater in the 1960's; its first profes-

sional production was by the Old Vic Theatre Com-
[108] pany at the Liverpool Playhouse on 31 October 1945.

4

The second volume of O'Casey's autobiography, *Pictures in the Hallway*, covering the years 1892–1905, had been completed in the first half of 1941. It was published by Macmillans of London in 1942 and was promptly banned by the Irish Censorship of Publications Board. Meanwhile he was starting his notes for the third volume, *Drums Under the Window*, which deals with the period 1905–16. At the same time he was engaged in writing his next play, *Red Roses For Me*.

The national rail strike of 1911, a strike that affected both British and Irish railways, provided the background for his new play, and not – as has been frequently stated – the better known lockout of 1913. In May 1956 O'Casey wrote in a programme note for a production of the play at the University of California at Los Angeles: 'The play doesn't deal with the Lock-Out, but with a strike of Railwaymen of the British Isles long before Jim Larkin was known to Irish workers.' This is not quite accurate, as O'Casey attached two incidents to the 1911 strike, both relating to the later lockout, namely the men's demand for an extra shilling a week and the meeting in Sackville (O'Connell) Street, when Larkin was arrested and a police baton-charge resulted in at least one death and some four hundred people, as well as sixty police, injured. Moreover, Larkin formed the Irish Transport and General Workers' Union in 1909, and Seán himself was a member of it at the time of the strike. However, in other respects the play fully supports O'Casey's statement. Both the leading character,

Ayamonn Breydon, and Roory O'Balacaun, the zealous Irish-Irelander, are railway employees, as was Seán himself; the two railwaymen in the second act make it clear that it is their strike that is proclaimed by the authorities, while Foster and Dowzard, the blacklegs, or 'scabs' as they were called at the time, are railway foremen. It may seem strange that these two characters are portrayed as Orangemen from the North of Ireland; but, as Alan Simpson has recently pointed out,[35] many of the employees of the Great Northern Railway Company, for which Seán himself worked, were recruited in Belfast and were living in the same quarter of the city as the Caseys at this time. As Protestants these Northerners usually occupied senior posts, presumably being considered more reliable than the local Catholic workers.

Red Roses is clearly an autobiographical play. Many of the characters and incidents occur in *Pictures in the Hallway* and *Drums Under the Window*. Ayamonn is, of course, a highly idealised portrait of the playwright at a time when he was still a devout member of the Church of Ireland and his sympathies with the Labour movement were being aroused. We see him with his passion for Shakespeare and his interests in painting and songwriting and his voracious appetite for books. His mother is portrayed in Mrs Breydon with her charitable missions and her beloved window-sill flowers. The character of Sheila Mavourneen is based on Seán's early love for the Catholic Maura Keating. The Rev. E. Clinton is, as pointed out earlier, a kindly reminder of Seán's friend, the Rector of St Barnabas, who, like the clergyman in the play, faced strong opposition from the low-church fundamentalist Orangemen of his select vestry. The characters of Roory O'Balacaun and Mulcanny, the 'mocker of all things sacred', are both based on Seán's friends, as well as representing respectively the narrow nationalist and atheistic Darwinian views circulating during this [110] period of his life. Finally, the bagpipes that accompany the bearers of Ayamonn's body in the last act are reminders of Seán's work as one of the founders of the St Laurence O'Toole Pipers' Band.

The great transformation scene of the third act, when the city is bathed in a miraculous sunset and the hawkers and loungers on a bridge over the Liffey are inspired by Ayamonn's words to pledge themselves to build 'a fair city', 'free from hunger and hardship', had its origin in an incident recounted in *Pictures in the Hallway* when the young John Casside/Casey gazes in wonder at a sunset over the Liffey and vows 'to be strong; to stand out among many; to quit himself like a man.'[36]

Red Roses may be ranked with *The Silver Tassie* and *Cock-a-Doodle Dandy* as the best of O'Casey's plays written in exile. Its subject, the awakening of the poor, the hopeless, the downtrodden to a brighter future that is theirs by right – 'Sons and daughters of princes are we all, an' one with th' race of Milesius!' – was ever a theme to draw forth the full flowering of O'Casey's rhetoric. In Ayamonn's vision of a future Dublin the language swells up like the final movement of Beethoven's 'Choral' Symphony till it breaks into song:

> Fair city, I tell thee, our souls shall not
> slumber
> Within th' warm beds of ambition and
> gain;
> Our hands shall stretch out to th' fullness
> of labour,
> Till wonder an' beauty within thee shall
> reign. . . .

But it must also be said that in the later plays O'Casey's striving for heightened effect can smother the dramatic impulse of the dialogue with a pseudo-literary artifice that blunts its purpose, as for instance in the following passage where Sheila berates Ayamonn for offering shelter to the atheist Mulcanny:

> *Sheila (with quiet bitterness):* Well, shelter him, then, that by right should be lost in the night, a black night, an' bitterly lonely, without a dim ray from a half-hidden star to give him a far-away companionship; ay, an' a desolate rest under a thorny and dripping thicket of lean and twisted whins, too tired to thry to live longer against th' hate of the black wind an' th' grey rain. Let him lie there, let him live there, forsaken, forgotten by all who live under a kindly roof and close to a cosy fire!

O'Casey's inability to get his plays produced before they were published could sometimes result in passages that were over-written for stage purposes, as well as flaws of construction, requiring editing and reshaping by sympathetic direction.

Red Roses, like *The Star Turns Red*, reflects O'Casey's dream of the eventual triumph of Communism, but the aggression of the earlier play is here softened and humanised. Abstract characters, such as the Purple Priest and Red Jim, are replaced by men and women of flesh and blood. In its mixture of symbolism and realism the play achieves what O'Casey was striving for in *The Silver Tassie*. The form of both plays is similar: both have their expressionist scenes and their theme-songs from which they take their titles; but their messages are fundamentally different. *The Silver Tassie* reflects the pessimist philosophy of the post-war twenties in the fatalism of the war-crippled footballer and his blinded companion. *Red Roses*, on the other hand, presents an act of faith in the enlightened spirit of the young and in the future as symbolised in its theme-song:

A sober black shawl hides her body entirely,
[112] Touch'd be the sun an' th' salt spray of th' sea;
But down in th' darkness a slim hand, so lovely,
Carries a rich bunch of red roses for me!

5

For the first time in seventeen years an O'Casey play was given its world première in his native city. On 15 March 1943 *Red Roses For Me* was presented at the Olympia Theatre, Dublin, directed by Shelah Richards, the original Nora Clitheroe of *The Plough and the Stars*. A subsequent revival of the play at the Gaiety Theatre, Dublin, was to result in the breach between O'Casey and his Dublin 'butty', Gabriel Fallon. Fallon's review of the play in *The Standard*, a Catholic paper that had consistently attacked O'Casey, and of which Fallon was now the drama critic, brought an abrupt end to their friendship.[37]

On 26 February 1946 *Red Roses* was presented by Bronson Albery at the Embassy Theatre, Swiss Cottage, at that time the leading 'try-out' theatre for West End productions. The press was encouraging. 'Mr O'Casey writes with superb Elizabethan energy, using the language of the Dublin streets, and the language of the Irish poets to comic or to tragic ends, swinging it to a rhythm which is all his own,' wrote the critic of *The Times*. The play was transferred to the New Theatre, St Martin's Lane, and later to Wyndham's Theatre. Seán came to London to see it, his first visit for seven years. His eyesight, Eileen recalls, had now seriously deteriorated, and he could no longer move freely around. A consultation with his eye specialist produced a depressing report: it was now clear that he would eventually lose his sight completely. Nevertheless, this does not seem to have slowed down his work. *Drums Under the*

Window was finished in July 1944, and in February of that year he wrote to Nathan that he 'might start on a play, possibly a war-play – that's how my thoughts go at the moment'.[38] On 22 November the manuscript of *Oak Leaves and Lavender* was sent to his publishers.

If *Red Roses For Me* is possibly the best of his exile plays, *Oaks Leaves and Lavender* is the least good. O'Casey himself acknowledged it as a failure in a letter written on 28 May 1947 to his son Breon: 'I myself have left more failures behind me (what others called failures) than I bother to sit down to count. Even today, I leave behind me the failure of *Oak Leaves and Lavender*, having learned a lot from it which I hope may serve me in the future.'[39]

By the end of 1941 America had entered the war, and Seán felt justified in giving his full support to Britain's war effort now that his two favourite nations – the USSR and the USA – had engaged in the struggle against the Fascist powers. Despite her powerful allies, Britain was still fighting for her life against the nightly destruction of her cities and airfields by the *Luftwaffe*; her only effective means of defence the little force of Spitfires – truly a David – and – Goliath situation. It was this heroic struggle – soon to be known as the Battle of Britain – in which a pilot's life was not expected to exceed eight weeks, that Seán set out to portray in his new play. In a letter to the Macmillan Company of New York he described it as 'an O'Casey tribute to the big fight waged here [England] against Nazi domination'.

The scene is laid in a large room of an English manor-house whose chatelaine, Dame Hatherleigh, is a firm believer in the British-Israelite movement. Her son, Edgar, and her Irish butler's son, Drishogue, both newly commissioned RAF pilots, are paired off with Monica, the daughter of a local farmer, and Jessie,

a land girl. Both young men perish in their first sortie.
[114] Jessie dies in an attempt to rescue Edgar from his burning plane, while Monica discloses that she is to bear a child by Drishogue. The play reveals O'Casey's weaknesses: heavy-handed symbolism – much of it too obscure to register in a stage performance – mawkish love-making, crude melodrama and incidents unrelated to the plot. With the exception of the Irish butler, Felim Feelim O'Morrigun, the major characters are unworthy of Seán's genius, and his attempt to use Cornish dialect for his comic characters robs them of much of the O'Casey richness and humour.

The play was first produced at the Staatsteater, Helsingbors, Sweden, on 28 November 1946. (O'Casey's later plays were often better appreciated by continental theatre managers than by their American and British counterparts.) In the following year it was presented in London by Bronson Albery at the Lyric Theatre, Hammersmith, after a try-out week in Eastbourne. Seán attended the final rehearsals. He was bitterly disappointed with the direction and staging, and returned to Totnes before the play opened in London. Eileen was present on the opening night, 18 May 1947, accompanied by Breon, who had recently been called up for military service. She wrote: 'It was – so poorly directed – only a ghost of Seán's work. . . . We felt strange and embarassed; during the intervals, not wishing to talk to anyone, we disappeared to our several cloakrooms until the curtain rose again.'[40] Seán too, in *Sunset and Evening Star*, has some harsh things to say:

> Whenever he ventured to think of what was the worst production of a play of his, his heart's blood pressed into his head and all the world became red. . . . Never before had Seán seen such an assumed and massive incompetency in a pro-

> ducer assigned to the English theatre. . . . The play, admittedly, was a difficult one, possibly even a bad one, but the shocking production failed, in every possible way, to show whether it was one, or all, of these, failed to give the slightest guidance to the experimental playwright.[41]

The first edition of *Oak Leaves and Lavender* was subtitled 'A Warld on Wallpaper' – a punning reference to Yeats's criticism of *The Silver Tassie* (the word 'warld' being a telescoping of 'world' and 'war'). It was dedicated: 'To little Johnny Grayburn who, in his sailor suit, played football with me on a Chalfont lawn and afterwards gallantly fell in the battle of Arnhem'. Lieutenant Grayburn was posthumously awarded the Victoria Cross.

> And what have you left of yourself behind for coming life to see, to honour, and admire? A blink o' scarlet ribbon holding up a copper cross, with a golden centre. Not enough, not enough, Johnny Grayburn; not enough to pay for your sturdy body, your handsome face, the promise of the future man. I was very fond of you, Johnny Grayburn, for you were all that a youngster ought to be; the makings of a fine, intelligent, colourful human being. . . . So strong, so sure of life, so sure of fame, maybe; so sure of his own boyish pride, so sure that God was with him. The day of his youth was the day of his glory; and that day passed off into everlasting darkness.[42]

7
Sunset and Evening Star

1

On 7 May the war in Europe came to an end. Seán watched from his garden gate as Eileen and the five-year-old Shivaun, 'joined by all people able to walk, children as well, with some babies wheeled in prams', wended their way in a torchlight procession through the town of Totnes, 'singing lustily the songs that were popular in the war years'.[1]

A new life began, a life that provided greater social justice but rapidly lost the togetherness, the humour, and grim determination of wartime Britain. The lights went on again; the nightly fears were ended; but rationing continued, and young men were still called up for military service, Breon O'Casey among them. Seán was at work writing the fourth volume of his autobiography, *Inishfallen Fare Thee Well*, beginning with a moving account of his mother's death, 'Mrs Casside Takes a Holiday', and ending with his departure from Ireland in 1926. The completed manuscript was sent to Macmillans in April 1947. Its publication in 1949 was to earn him the Page One Award of the Newspaper Guild of New York – 'a superb work by a writer too little recognised in this country'. In Ireland, where the first two volumes of the autobiography had been banned by the Censorship Board, it provoked a storm of protest as being 'insultingly anti-Irish and anti-Catholic'. In replying to a favourable review in the *Sunday Times* in which the critic

Desmond MacCarthy remarked on O'Casey's loathing of the Church of Rome, Seán wrote:

> I don't really loathe the Roman Catholic Church. That is a wide term, embracing all the souls baptised into its communion, and even those baptised outside it. . . . I loathe those who are turning her liturgy into vulgar nonsense and her temples into dens of thieves. . . . No intelligent man could possibly loathe the dogmas embedded in the 'deposit of faith left by the apostles'. The idea of the incarnation, the ascent, the coming of the paraclete, and all the moral philosophy, the poetic tales concerned with these, are beautiful; and, though not accepted either in substance or in fact, remain beautiful, and I am not one to loathe the lovely.[2]

Nevertheless, in his next three major plays, as well as in his short satiric ones, both Ireland and the Church come in for some rough handling. In them he returns from his voyage into the past to take a hard look at contemporary Ireland: the narrow-mindedness of the priest-ridden state with its acquisitive materialism, its bourgeois pretentions, its lip-homage to the national ideals that it had effectively discarded. To these Seán opposes the ideals of youth, of joyful, uninhibited sex, and of that fullness of life that Ayamonn in *Red Roses For Me* saw in his vision of the city of the future.

In these final plays Dublin is no longer the necessary location of the action; rather he chooses to place them in mythical country villages and towns bearing fictional names, such as Nyadnanave, Ballybeedhust, Doonavale and Kylenamoe in the county of Melloe. In this mythical and pastoral world fantasy can reign supreme. A gigantic Cock can bring about strange happenings; a plaster saint can blow blasts on his 'buckineeno'; women can sprout horns; 'Le Petit

Pisseur' can desert his Brussels fountain to wreak [118] havoc on the morals of the inhabitants of a Dublin suburb. O'Casey's love of laughter, of the joy of living, of dance and song and story was never so ebullient, but behind the fantasy and the farce lies a spirit of profound disillusion. He seems to despair that Ireland will ever be cured of the social ills, bred of clerical oppression and money-grubbing materialism, that were forcing her young sons and daughters to seek freedom overseas. It was a disillusion felt by many of Ireland's best writers in the priest-ridden de Valera years.

2

In the summer of 1947 O'Casey set to work on his next full-length play, *Cock-a-Doodle Dandy*. 'Once more', wrote Eileen, 'he sang a good deal; it was as if the rhythm, mostly Irish folk songs, helped his thoughts. I am sure he was excited because of his resolve to break with realism, not just in a single act, as in the war scene of *The Tassie*, but through an entire piece.'[3]

In a letter to Nathan, dated 10 September 1947, he explained that the play will 'hit at the present tendency in Éire to return to primitive beliefs, and Éire's tendency to puritanism. I hope it will be gay with a sombre thread of seriousness in it.'[4]

The 'primitive beliefs' refer to an incident in the play in which Julia, a young girl suffering from an incurable disease, seeks the aid of the miraculous powers of Lourdes, encouraged by the prayers of the whole village, only to return unhealed. Unrelated as it is to the plot, this incident seems to be dragged in to illustrate O'Casey's scorn of superstition, and the encouragement given to it by the Church. But 'gaiety' there is, and 'a sombre thread of seriousness' too, in the theme – so characteristic of the later plays – of material and philistine attitudes allied to the kill-joy puritanism of the Church in battle with the vital forces of youth. Material values are represented by the money-grubbing farmer, Michael Marthraun, and his disreputable business associate, Sailor Mahan, each trying to cheat the other, while the power of the Church takes the menacing form of Father Domineer, determined to keep women in a state of subjection and to stifle all mention and manifestation of sex, whether in books or human relations. Against these forces stands Loreleen, the daughter of Marthraun by a former marriage, who has recently returned from England. With her is her *alter ego*, a miraculous Cock, the symbol of fertility and 'the joyful spirit of active love'.

In the initial stages of the conflict the Cock uses his magic power to get the better of his opponents, creating havoc in Marthraun's house, clawing the holy pictures and Marthraun's top hat, raising a wind that whips the trousers off the Police Sergeant, causing cups to fly out of the window, whiskey to change its colour, and the flagstaff bearing the Irish flag to fall to the ground. Finally, the Cock kidnaps Father Domineer himself, who, however, returns on the back of a barnacle goose to exile Loreleen to England, whence she is followed by Marthraun's young wife, her maid, Marion, and Marion's lover, Robin Adair, the Messenger. The old and loveless are left to continue their empty existence in a village deprived of youth. To Marthraun's inquiry as to what the Messenger would advise him to do, Robin replies: 'Die. There is little else useful for the likes of you to do.'

In an article in the *New York Times* written in 1958, in which he referred to *Cock-a-Doodle Dandy* as his favourite play, Seán had this to say: 'It isn't the clergy alone who booh and bluster against the

joy of life. . . . Playwrights and poets have a share
[120] in squeezing the mind of men into visions of woe and great lamentation.'[5] He was almost certainly referring to Samuel Beckett and to what he called 'the Freudians of the theatre'. 'I have nothing to do with Beckett,' he wrote in 1956. 'He isn't in me; nor am I in him. I am not waiting for Godot to bring me life; I am out after life myself, even at the age I have reached.'[6] In 'The Bald Primaqueera', the last essay he wrote, he attacked the nihilism of Antonin Artaud and his disciples, and the negative attitude to life of such playwrights as Harold Pinter, David Rudkin, Joe Orton, and N. F. Simpson.[7] Although in his old age Seán suffered much from pain, blindness and the loss of those dear to him, he never gave way to despair, nor lost faith in the future of mankind.

> The world has many sour noises, the body is an open target for many invisible enemies; all hurtful, some venomous, like the accursed virus which can bite deeply into flesh and mind. It is full of disappointments, and too many of us have to suffer the loss of a beloved child, a wound that aches bitterly till our end comes. Yet, even so, each of us one time or another can ride a white horse, can have rings on our fingers and bells on our toes, and, if we keep our senses open to the scents, sounds and sights all around us, we shall have music wherever we go.[8]

As a writer too he endured many cruel disappointments. In England and the United States his attempts to enrich the theatre of his time by the introduction of forms other than the conventional too seldom received the benefit of first-class performance. In Ireland his later plays were howled down by the critics. Yet he never lost his laughter, nor did he fail to strike back.

> As a playwright I have received knocks when the hair was brown and the face young-looking; and [121] I'm still getting them when, as Yeats said, I am old and grey and full of tears. Well, not quite tears, for within me the laugh comes and goes and always comes again. As well, one can hit back and land, at times, many a gregorian slashing blow on the conk of him who tries to trip, or on one who aims a blow below the belt.[9]

It must have seemed to Seán that *Cock-a-Doodle Dandy* was to suffer the same neglect as others of his plays. It found no immediate market in the professional theatre, its first production being left once again to the amateurs, this time at the People's Theatre of Newcastle-upon-Tyne. It did not appear in New York until November 1958, when it ran for little more than a fortnight at the off-Broadway Carnegie Hall Playhouse. In London it was not until ten years after the play had first appeared in print that it was presented at the Royal Court in September 1959, directed by George Devine and designed by Seán Kenny.

Deprived in both his adopted and native countries of the professional skills by which he might test his constant search for new dramatic expression, Seán's creative powers were concentrated on his autobiographies. *Rose and Crown*, the fifth and penultimate volume, appeared in July 1952. It contains that splendidly theatrical dialogue between Seán and the confused but undaunted Stanley Baldwin at one of Lady Londonderry's 'at homes':

> Baldwin took a few meditative puffs [at his pipe], then renewed his valiant chatter.
>
> – Yeats, your poet, knows his people. The Selt is well outside the world of men. That's why your heroes are universally so renowned. You do well to

remember your heroes – Daniel O'Connell, T. P.
[122] O'Connor and Timothy Healy.

– Ay, and Mister McGilligan, the famous father of Dublin's wonderful Mary Anne, added Seán.

– Him, too, added Baldwin; all good Irishmen. You do well to remember them.

– Never fear, said Seán. They shall be remembered for ever. You certainly know a lot of Irish History, sir, said Seán, letting his eyes shine with approval.

– Not really, O'Casey, replied Baldwin; and Seán saw that the man felt flattered. A Prime Minister has little time for study. But I know some, O'Casey; I know some. I've actually heard of Tara. And the great man actually smiled.

Sunset and Evening Star, the last and best-selling volume of his autobiography, was published in 1954. It ends:

> Even here, even now, when the sun had set and the evening star was chastely touching the bosom of the night, there were things to say, things to do. A drink first! What would he drink to – the past, the present, the future? To all of them! Here with whitened hair, desires failing, strength ebbing out of him, with the sun gone down, and with the serenity and calm warning of the evening star left to him, he drank to Life, to all it had been, to what it was, and to what it would be. Hurrah!

3

Three one-act plays were written between 1949 and 1950: *Hall of Healing*, *Bedtime Story* and *Time To Go*. The first, 'A Sincerious Farce', was based on his childhood experiences attending Dublin's Poor Law Dispensary in North William Street and his memories of treatment in St Mark's Ophthalmic Hospital for

Accidents and Diseases of the Eye and Ear, both vividly described in the first volume of his autobiography.[10] In *Bedtime Story*, a light-hearted Feydeau-like farce, he portrayed the tribulations of a pious young Dubliner who invites a prostitute to his flat but is too mean to pay for her services. *Time to Go*, set in a small country town, repeats the theme of capitalist materialism allied to the power of the Church that Seán had explored in *Cock-a-Doodle Dandy*; like the earlier play, it makes use of symbolism and magic, though in this instance the magic is performed by human beings, the Widow Machree and 'Kelly from the Isle of Mananaun'. The play, with its background tune of 'Jingle Coins', should prove effective in performance, though its cast of thirteen players – too large for a one-act play – has so far proved a stumbling-block to professional production. *Time To Go* was first presented on 7 May 1952 in the Jugoslav-American Hall, New York. The only production in Britain was at the amateur Unity Theatre in London in May 1953.

In the following year the O'Caseys were again obliged to move, as their landlord required the house in Totnes for relatives. In June 1954 they established themselves in a flat in St Marychurch, outside Torquay and overlooking the sea. Once more Eileen was faced with the formidable problem of settling Seán – now in his seventy-fifth year – into his new room, struggling to get his massive collection of books into some sort of order before installing him.

> His room was never just sleeping quarters, somewhere to dress and undress; it was his home. The remainder of the flat was to wander in, but when Seán spoke of 'home' it was his room he meant, filled with his strong personality; overcoat and mackintosh and caps behind the door – never

in the hall – his boots, from which he changed into slippers immediately he came in, set in the same place beside the fire.[11]

On 21 June Seán sent his new play, *The Bishop's Bonfire*, to his publishers. Once again we find capitalism and the Church in alliance to keep the workers in subjection. Once again O'Casey introduces the need for the young to emigrate if they are to escape the narrow life and loveless marriages imposed on them by the materialist aims of their parents, supported by the Church. The action concerns the preparations for the visit of Bishop Bill Mullarkey to his home town, Ballyoonagh. The high point of the visit is to be the lighting of a bonfire in which 'piles of bad books an' evil pictures' are to be consumed in the flames. The Bishop's host, Councillor O'Reiligan, the richest man in the district, recently appointed a papal count, together with the parish priest, Canon Burren, is preparing to give the Bishop, once a wild lad with a patch on the seat of his pants, a royal welcome. The preparations are hopelessly frustrated by O'Reiligan's totally incompetent but wholly delightful workmen. The sub-plot concerns the love affairs of the Councillor's two daughters, Keelin, a warm-hearted and lively girl attached to a timid workman, Daniel Coolcoohy, and her pious sister, Foorawn, who has stifled her love for a spoiled priest, Manus Moanroe, so as to lead a life of nun-like celibacy. The play contains none of O'Casey's positive philosophy, and the message that emerges is one of disillusion over Ireland's future: in the words of Father Boheroe, one of O'Casey's enlightened priests, to Keelin and her timorous lover, Daniel,

> You've escaped from the dominion of the Big House with the Lion and the Unicorn on its front; don't let yourselves sink beneath the meaner

dominion of the big shop with the cross and shamrock on its gable.

Its ending is crudely melodramatic. Foorawn is shot by her lover when she surprises him in the act of stealing a bundle of notes to pay his fare to England. Father Burren and O'Reiligan manage to break the affair between Keelin and Daniel. The despotic alliance between the Church and capitalism has driven out the young from Ireland or forced them into submission, while the workers are too credulous to revolt against their oppressors.

'*The Bishop's Bonfire*', O'Casey declared to the critic of *The Times*, 'is a play about the ferocious chastity of the Irish, a lament for the condition of Ireland, which is an apathetic country now, losing all her energy, enthusiasm and resolution.'[12] The only positive characters are Keelin, who escapes to England, and Father Boheroe. However, once again the pessimism of the theme is allayed by O'Casey's unerring sense of comedy and his genius at providing good acting parts, particularly in his non-didactic characters. In the Codger, an eighty-four-year-old boozer and rhymer, he has provided one of his most superb comic characters, a true descendant of Captain Boyle and Fluther Good, that could not fail to attract Cyril Cusack when he applied for the rights of the play with a Dublin production in view. On 28 February 1955 it appeared at the Gaiety Theatre, directed by Tyrone Guthrie.

Ten days before the first night *The Standard*, a Catholic weekly, launched a campaign against O'Casey. Photographs of excerpts from the autobiographies intended to illustrate his anti-Catholicism appeared on its front page. This was followed by a further article intended to inflame hostility against the production. 'It is one of the contradictions of modern life', thundered *The Standard*, 'tha he should be offered a stage in the capital city of th country most steadfastly ranged against the enemie who are his friends. . . . Where is the native self respect?'[13]

As a result, hours before the curtain rose on th first night some two thousand people jammed th streets outside the Gaiety, pleading for standing roon in the solidly booked theatre. Meanwhile police car brought more and more reinforcements to prevent a riot. Seán was too ill to attend, but Eileen was there with Shivaun. So was Gabriel Fallon, Seán's erstwhile friend, now one of his sternest critics. In the *Evening Press* Fallon wrote: 'I set it down with regret that however much *The Bishop's Bonfire* blazed in the imagination of Mr O'Casey, the dramatic fire that burned *Juno* and *The Plough* into an incandescent of greatness is now a handful of grey dust.' The other press reactions were mixed. Séamus Kelly in the *Irish Times* concluded his review with 'Positively the worst play I have ever had to sit through.' The British critics were more kindly. 'It succeeds beyond the hopes of its enemies. It fails a little more than O'Casey's friends would wish,' wrote Gerard Fay in the *Manchester Guardian*. Its success with Dublin audiences, however, was not in doubt. The run was extended by two weeks, eventually being forced to give way to a previously booked season of opera.

In *The Green Crow*, a collection of his occasional writings, together with three short stories, O'Casey defended the play against those who maintained it was untrue to Irish life. To those critics who declared he was out of touch with Ireland he replied:

> I know the mind of Ireland because I am within it; I know the heart of Ireland because I am one of its corners; I know the five senses of Ireland because I

> am within them and they within me; they bid me look, and when I look, I see; they bid me listen, and when I listen, I hear.[14]

The 'Green Crow' of the title is a portrait of O'Casey himself. It is, as David Krause points out,

> a very significant portrait because it highlights the two essential impulses that have motivated him throughout his life – the mock-heroic and the heroic, the satire laughter and the visionary faith. The Green Crow is a complex old bird, the most uncommon of common birds. He can be gay and gregarious, proud and lonely. He is capable of profound hope and faith, but he has seldom shown charity towards his enemies. He loves a jest for its own sake, yet he also sees laughter as a weapon against evil. He can mock all aspects of life that displease him, but behind the anti-heroic laughter of the crow there is the heroic faith of an artist who envisions a better world.[15]

The same volume contained two of O'Casey's articles on Shaw, a token of his lifelong admiration for his fellow-Dubliner. Shaw died in October 1950. Two days before his death he had said to Eileen: 'If there is an Almighty, Eileen, I'll have a lot of questions to ask him.'[16]

The Green Crow was published in America in 1956 and in London in 1957. When copies of the British edition were sent to Ireland they were impounded by the Irish customs without explanation. It was a year before this mysterious ban was lifted.

In February 1956 Seán was undergoing a prostate operation in Torbay Hospital. A month later a more serious condition arose when a stone developed in his kidney. An operation was considered necessary; severe bronchitis followed. For three months visitors, other

than members of the family, were forbidden. Christ-
[128] mas of that year was to bring a tragedy to the O'Caseys that no length of years could erase. Their younger son, Niall, who was studying at the London School of Economics, came home for the vacation in the second week of December. He was tired and seemingly run down. On 29 December he died of leukemia. Seán wrote his lament:

> I cry a caoine for my Niall, for though I may bear it like a man, I must also feel it like a man, and cannot feel ashamed that my sigh will be in the winds that blow where'er his dear ashes blow, for he had very gentle, loving ways within him; but the caoine, as he would wish, goes out for all the golden lads and girls whose lovely rose of youth hath perished in its bud.[17]

Although nearing blindness and often in pain, the great 'Blaster and Blighter', as Shaw had called him, rose above the heartbreak. In May of the following year he wrote to Nathan: 'To keep my mind from brooding over our boy, I have set out to try to write a comedy, with my head among the clouds rather than the stars; a play of common language, but, I hope with some humour in it. It's called "The Night is Whispering".'[18] It was later to be called *The Drums of Father Ned*.

4

From the beginning of the 1960s the winds of change blowing from overseas began to sweep away some of the barriers, taboos and frustrations, that had kept Catholic Ireland apart from the post-war world. When de Valera quitted active politics in 1959 to occupy the post of President, younger brains were brought into government. Under the pragmatic leadership of

Seán Lemass, an era of economic expansion began. Foreign capital was encouraged, foreign industries were established, and the country began to benefit from an ever-increasing tourist industry.

In the Church itself a new era was dawning with the brief but revolutionary reign of Pope John XXIII. Despite the rigid conservatism of the Irish hierarchy, typified by the powerful Archbishop of Dublin, the Most Rev. Dr J. C. McQuaid, many of the younger priests were taking an active interest in social change. As Ireland increasingly became a member of the European community the emancipated and progressive elements no longer felt the need to emigrate. If Seán did not live to see the full effect of these changes, he at least sensed the shape of things to come in his new play.

The Drums of Father Ned cannot be counted among his best plays, but it is the most prophetic. The theme is the familiar one, the revolt of vigorous youth against the stranglehold of the clergy and that of the hypocritical materialistic bourgeoisie. The time is the present, but the play opens with a 'Prerumble' set in the days of the Black and Tans, in which Binnington, a Free Stater, and McGilligan, a Republican, who – despite the fact that they were brought up together – have not spoken to each other for years, prefer to be shot rather than shake hands. In deciding to release them, the British Black and Tan officer senses that 'they will do more harm to Ireland living, than they'll ever do to Ireland dead'. The action then moves forward to the present. The small town of Doonavale is feverishly preparing for a Tostal (festival). The two enemies are now prominent and prosperous citizens: Binnington is mayor of the town; his rival and enemy, McGilligan, is deputy mayor. Although still not on speaking terms in their social life, in matters of making money 'business is business'! The Church is represented by another of O'Casey's kill-joy priests, Father [130] Fillifogue, differing little from his predecessors in his attitude to the young. The young, too, mainly conform to O'Casey's stereotypes. They are the son and daughter of the two old enemies. Both are determined to oppose Father Fillifogue and those who protest at the revelry that is to be their contribution to the festival. 'Our Blessed Lord', Nora McGilligan declares, would have been pleased with this celebration:

> If He didn't dance himself, He must have watched the people at it, and, maybe, clapped His hands when they did it well. He must have often listened to the people singin', and been caught up with the rhythm of the gentle harp and psalter, and His feet may have tapped the ground along with the gayer sthrokes of the tabor and the sounds of the cymbles tinkling.

But there are two important differences in these young people's attitude from that of the previous generation: they are not afraid to admit that they sleep together, and they have no intention of escaping from Ireland. On the contrary, they will stand for election for mayor and deputy mayor, and for the Dáil itself. 'We're fighting what is old and stale and vicious, the hate, the meanness their policies preach.' The instrument of this new fighting attitude is none other than a priest – the red-haired, green-eyed Father Ned. We never see him, but the sound of his drum grows louder and more menacing as the old values are ridiculed and eroded and the victory of young Ireland approaches.

In October 1957 the Dublin Tostal Council accepted the play with delight. It was planned to present it as part of the Theatre Festival to be held in the spring of the following year, together with *Bloomsday*, Alan McLellan's dramatisation of James Joyce's *Ulysses*, and three mime plays by Beckett. This was a challenge to the censorious attitude of the Church towards all three writers – a challenge which the old guard could not let pass. On 10 January the *Irish Times* announced:

> For the past week there has been some doubt as to whether these two plays [*Father Ned* and *Bloomsday*] would be part of the Festival programme. Last week the Council became aware that the Most Rev. Dr McQuaid, Archbishop of Dublin, did not approve of their inclusion. As a result of their inclusion, this year's Tostal will not be marked by an official Mass.

For a time the Tostal Council held to their decision to present the plays, but the Archbishop's disapproval – he had not read them – would have had serious repercussions, especially in obtaining finance for future operations of the Tostal. When the Dublin Council of Trades Unions announced its support for the Archbishop's action, the Council gave way. Their method of doing so was hardly commendable. O'Casey received a letter from the producing management, stating that the play's 'structural state made it unproduceable' and requesting his permission for the management to make such changes as were required. As a veteran dramatist Seán O'Casey could not accept such an insult. Not only did he refuse, but he banned the professional production of any of his plays by Dublin companies. This was a blow that struck hardest at the Abbey Theatre, an innocent victim of the whole affair. The ban was not lifted until 1964, when the Abbey was invited to present *Juno and the Paycock* and *The Plough and the Stars* at the Aldwych Theatre, London, as the Irish contribution to the four-hundredth celebration of Shakespeare's birth.

Some compensation for this blow to O'Casey's pride came at the end of the year 1957 when *Cock-*

a-Doodle Dandy and *The Shadow of a Gunman* were presented in New York, the former in the off-Broadway Carnegie Hall, the latter in the Bijou Theatre. Seán was too frail to accept an invitation to attend, but Eileen went: a much-deserved break for a valiant woman who had sacrificed not only her career but all those things she loved so much – the company of friends, concerts, theatres and art galleries.

5

By the mid-1950s money was more plentiful. Seán's autobiographies were selling well, particularly in America. The first two volumes of the autobiographies were filmed as *Young Casside*. The screen play was written by John Whiting, but despite a distinguished cast including Rod Taylor, Julie Christie, Michael Redgrave, Edith Evans, Flora Robson and Maggie Smith, the result was disappointing. Two other films were made during the 1950s: *Seán O'Casey*, originally a National Broadcasting Company television programme entitled *A Conversation with Seán O'Casey*, and Paul Rotha's film of the Abbey Theatre, *Cradle of Genius*, which included a conversation between Seán and his old friend, Barry Fitzgerald, brought especially from Hollywood to Seán's great delight.

In 1959 Sean wrote to Ronald Ayling: 'I've just finished a satiric fantasy – short two-scened – dedicated to "Ireland's ferocious chastity", called *Figuro in the Night*.'[19] The play was first produced at the Hofstra University Playhouse, New York, on 4 May 1962, and its first professional production took place in October of the same year at New York's Theatre de Lys. The play relates the erotic effect of the miraculous arrival from Brussels of 'Le Petit Pisseur' upon a crowd attending a fair in O'Connell Street,

Dublin. It is short in action, but it reflects in ritual and symbolic form the arid, loveless life of the old in contrast to the new and vital life of the young. This new life is not confined to Dublin: a bird-like lad appears (Angus, the Celtic God of Love) to announce that Figuro is appearing everywhere in Ireland. The play's themesong, based on the traditional air 'Oh dear, what can the matter be? Johnny's so long at the fair', appeals for a less inhibited approach to sex in Ireland.

> My Johnny, he wanted to stay here and mind
> me.
> But in what state o' dress would me ma 'n' da
> find me?
> They'd hustle me into me room, an' then bind
> me,
> When they hurried me home from the fair.

Grean fun too is his one-act play *The Moon Shines on Kylenamoe*, first staged at the Theatre de Lys in harness with *Figuro in the Night*. This is vintage O'Casey farce, carrying no social or political message. The action concerns a bewildered British Foreign Office official, arriving in the middle of the night at the deserted railway halt of Kylenamoe, 'a village consisting of a general store and thirty houses, fourteen of them empty'. He is the bearer of an important message for his Prime Minister, who is holidaying in the local manor-house. The fearful difficulties he encounters in trying to hire transport to take him to his destination while the train crew and the local porter-cum-station-master argue the pros and cons of the situation provide half an hour of pure entertainment.

Vintage O'Casey farce is also to be found in the opening scene of his last play, *Behind the Green Curtains*, where two old and somewhat intoxicated hawkers, Lizzie Latterly and Angela Carrigeen, dis-

cuss the superior benefits to be obtained from pray-
[134] ing to the 'Blesseds' as compared with the 'Saints'. A saint 'gets kinda stuck-up, y' know', whereas 'a Blessed buzzes down, all ears, the minuite he hears his name mentioned'. The play is a satire on the cowardice and hypocrisy of certain Catholic intellectuals, afraid to go against the dictates of the hierarchy and hiding behind their green curtains of false piety and patriotism. It was first produced in December 1962 at the University of Rochester, New York State.

Seán's last publication during his lifetime was *Under a Colored Cap*, a collection of essays and articles, nearly all of which were written in the late 1950s and 1960s. It contains his moving lament on the death of his son, 'Under a Greenwood Tree He Died'. The title of the book refers to his collection of colored (he prefers the American spelling) caps, or 'beanos', given to him by friends and admirers from all over the world.

On 30 March 1960 Seán celebrated his eightieth birthday. Telegrams, cablegrams and birthday greetings reached him from all over the world, as well as a host of flowers, among them bunches of red roses. In the following year Ireland at last recognised the genius of her wayward son when Trinity College offered him an honorary doctorate. Seán was grateful, but found it impossible to accept. 'Seán O'Casey, Litt.D.! No, Sir, this would never do. I am a wandering minstrel singing his share of songs at the corners of occasional streets: such I was, such I am, and such I shall die!'[20]

During these latter years his main activity was concentrated on his voluminous correspondence, which, ever since his departure from Ireland, had grown in volume: public letters to newspapers and journals in Ireland, America, England and Russia; private letters to people of all nations and of all ages. David Krause, the painstaking editor of his letters, has pointed out that since O'Casey was deprived of a regular theatre audience for his plays, his letter-writing became 'an urgent and compensatory need; the hundreds of people all over the world with whom he exchanged letters became his own private audience, his intimate and immediate contact with everyday reality'.[21]

In his last years, when his eyesight had nearly gone, his letters had to be read to him, as well as his replies; for, although he could touch-type, he was unable to read what he had written. Usually this task fell to Eileen; she also read the daily papers to him, and in the evenings his favourite books, especially Shakespeare's sonnets and the familiar and much-loved passages from the plays that he could still quote by heart. 'It was dreadful to see him there among the books he could not read . . . [though] by putting one slant-wise to his good eye he could sometimes make out a word or two.'[22] Nevertheless, even now his fighting spirit never wavered.

On 12 September 1964 he sent his last article, 'The Bald Primaqueera', to the *Atlantic Monthly* in New York. In August of that year he had suffered a heart attack coupled with acute bronchitis and for two unhappy weeks was confined to bed in Torbay Hospital. When he returned to the flat he became increasingly tired. Eileen was acutely worried by the threatened sale of their house following the death of their landlord, fearing that if they had to move, Seán would never be able to find his way around the furniture and his spirit would be broken. He was spared this blow to his proud and independent spirit. On 18 September 1964, 'between the sunset and the evening star', he died. Perhaps Tennyson's great hymn, from which he took the title of the last volume of his life-story, best expressed his wish:

Sunset and evening star,
[136] And one clear call for me!
And may there be no meaning of the bar
When I put out to sea,
But such a tide as moving seems to sleep,
Too full for sound and foam,
When that which drew from out the boundless deep
Turns again home.

References

Prerumble (pp. 1–7)

1. *Letters of Seán O'Casey*, Vol. I: *1910–1941*, ed. D. Krause, 268.
2. D. Krause, 'A Self-Portrait of the Artist as a Man' in Ayling, ed., *Seán O'Casey: Modern Judgments*, 235.
3. *Letters*, 637.
4. R. Mooney, 'Playwright in Exile' in Mikhail and O'Riordan, *The Sting and the Twinkle*, 72.
5. *I Knock at the Door*, 1939; *Pictures in the Hallway*, 1942; *Drums Under the Window*, 1945; *Inishfallen Fare Thee Well*, 1949; *Rose and Crown*, 1952; *Sunset and Evening Star*, 1954.

Chapter 1: Johnny Casey (pp. 8–22)

1. *I Knock at the Door*, 38.
2. *Pictures in the Hallway*, 131.
3. *Lady Gregory's Journals*, 72.
4. Krause, *Seán O'Casey and his World*, 9.
5. Quoted in Greaves, *Seán O'Casey: Politics and Art*, 22.
6. A. Butler, 'The Early Background' in McCann, ed., *The World of Seán O'Casey*, 21.
7. Kit (Christopher) Casey, 'The O'Casey I Knew', *ibid.*, 164–5.
8. S. McCann, 'The Girl He Left Behind', *ibid.*, 32–3.
9. *Pictures in the Hallway*, 59.
10. Margulies, *The Early Life of Seán O'Casey*, 28–9; Greaves, 30. Both authors question the veracity of this incident. Greaves points out its similarity to the beating administered to Stephen Dedalus in Joyce's *A Portrait of the Artist as a Young Man*. If, however, it did occur, it was almost certainly at St Barnabas's School and not, as stated by O'Casey, at St Mary's.
11. *I Knock at the Door*, 112.
12. *Ibid.*, 264–5.

13. *Pictures in the Hallway*, 25–9; Krause, *Seán O'Casey and his World*, 10, identifies Tommie Talton with the playwright Louis D'Alton, Charles's son, who was, however, not yet born.
14. *Pictures in the Hallway*, 201.
15. *Ibid.*, 203.
16. *Observer*, 6 Mar. 1929.
17. *Evening Standard*, 5 Mar. 1926.
18. Kit Casey in McCann, ed., 165.
19. *Ibid.*, 11.

Chapter 2: Seán Ó Cathasaigh (pp 23–41)

1. *Drums Under the Window*, 4.
2. E. Blythe, *Trasna na Bóinne*, Dublin 1958, 85.
3. Holloway, *Impressions*, 229.
4. *Drums Under the Window*, 22.
5. *Ibid.*, 94–5.
6. *Ibid.*, 220.
7. *Ibid.*, 232–3.
8. *Letters*, 34.
9. *Ibid.*, 698.
10. *Drums Under the Window*, 297.
11. *Ibid.*, 305.
12. *Ibid.*, 323–5.
13. *Inishfallen Fare Thee Well*, 46–7. This statement is denied by members of the family.
14. *Ibid.*, 61.
15. *Ibid.*, 299.
16. *Songs of the Wren* and *More Songs of the Wren*, both Dublin 1918, published by Fergus O'Connor, who had also published O'Casey's first book, *The Story of Thomas Ashe*.
17. *Windfalls*, London 1934.
18. Fallon, *Seán O'Casey: The Man I Knew*, 37.
19. *Letters*, 91–2.
20. *Lady Gregory's Journals*, 72–3.
21. *Letters*, 102–3.
22. *Ibid.*, 104–5.
23. *Poblacht na hÉireann*, 29 Mar. 1922. Cowasjee, *Seán O'Casey: The Man Behind the Plays*, 25, gives the name of the play as *The Robe of Rosheen* and states that the original story was published in *The Plain People*; this information, although supplied by O'Casey himself in a letter to Cowasjee, is erroneous.
24. *Letters*, 101.

25. Holloway, 218.
26. *Ibid.*, 227.

Chapter 3: Seán O'Casey (pp. 42–55)

1. *Lady Gregory's Journals*, 71.
2. Fallon, 5.
3. Greaves, 107.
4. Fallon, 13–14.
5. *Ibid.*, 14.
6. *Ibid.*, 16–17.
7. *Ibid.*, 17.
8. *Letters*, 132.
9. *Inishfallen Fare Thee Well*, 250–1. O'Casey wrongly places this incident after the production of *The Plough and the Stars.*
10. *Lady Gregory's Journals*, 88.
11. *Ibid.*, 91.
12. Fallon, 88.
13. *Letters*, 165–6.
14. Holloway, 251.
15. *Irish Times*, 12 Feb. 1926.
16. Fallon, 96–7.
17. *Inishfallen Fare Thee Well*, 387.
18. *Ibid.*, 249.

Chapter 4: Exile in London (pp. 56–72)

1. *Rose and Crown*, 5.
2. *Letters*, 189.
3. *Rose and Crown*, 29.
4. *The Poems of Wilfred Owen*, ed. E. Blunden, London 1931, 77.
5. *Letters*, 268.
6. *Ibid.*, 271.
7. *Ibid.*, 207.
8. E. O'Casey, *Eileen*, 83.
9. E. O'Casey, *Seán*, 79.
10. *Lady Gregory's Journals*, 104.
11. E. O'Casey, *Seán*, 82.
12. *Lady Gregory's Journals*, 106.
13. *Letters*, 239.
14. *Ibid.*, 240.
15. *Ibid.*, 284–5.
16. *Ibid.*, 368–9.
17. *Ibid.*, 369.
18. *Lady Gregory's Journals*, 124.

19. *Rose and Crown*, 130.
20. Fallon, 119.
21. M. H. Gaffney, OP, 'Dublin's Draught from *The Silver Tassie*', *Catholic Mind* (Sep. 1930).
22. E. O'Casey, *Eileen*, 129.

Chapter 5: Citizen of the World (pp. 73–92)

1. *The Flying Wasp*, 123.
2. *Ibid.*, 193–4.
3. S. O'Faolain, 'Ireland after Yeats', *The Bell* (summer 1953), quoted in Krause, *Seán O'Casey: The Man and his Work*, 44–5.
4. *Rose and Crown*, 80.
5. Greaves, 136.
6. Quoted in Cowasjee, 138.
7. *New York Times*, 26 Jan. 1934.
8. *Letters*, 445.
9. *Ibid.*, 460, 463.
10. *Irish Times*, 11 Oct. 1932.
11. *Letters*, 432–4.
12. *Ibid.*, 491–502.
13. *Rose and Crown*, 23.
14. *Letters*, 477.
15. *Ibid.*, 482.
16. Quoted in E. Coxhead, *Lady Gregory*, London 1961, 192.
17. A. and B. Gelb, *O'Neill*, New York 1962, 787–8.
18. *Letters*, 520–1.
19. *Rose and Crown*, 240–1.
20. *Letters*, 522.
21. *Rose and Crown*, 288.
22. *Ibid.*, 257.
23. *Boston Globe*, 17 Jan. 1935, quoted in *Letters*, 535n.
24. 'The Thing that Counts', *New Statesman*, 9 Feb. 1935, quoted in *Letters*, 537.
25. *Letters*, 541.
26. *Ibid.*, 576–7.
27. R. Speaight, 'In Defence of Seán O'Casey', *Catholic Herald*, 30 Aug. 1935.
28. *Rose and Crown*, 48.
29. 'Coward Codology: Noël Coward's Position as a Playwright', *Time and Tide*, 11 Jan. 1936.
30. *Letters*, 613.
31. *Ibid.*, 637.

Chapter 6: The Red Star and the Cross (pp. 93–115)

1. Cowasjee, 167.
2. *Letters*, 593.
3. Greaves, 142–3.
4. *Letters*, 646.
5. *Ibid.*, 753.
6. *Ibid.*, 731–2.
7. *Ibid.*, 652–3.
8. G. B. Shaw, *The Adventures of a Black Girl in her Search for God*, London 1932.
9. Krause, *Seán O'Casey and his World*, 146.
10. *Ibid.*, 145.
11. H. Macmillan, *Winds of Change*, London 1966, 187.
12. Greaves, 145.
13. *Letters*, 695–6.
14. *Ibid*, 705–27.
15. *Ibid.*, 731–52.
16. *I Knock at the Door*, 21–6.
17. *Ibid.*, 125–32.
18. *Drums Under the Window*, 237–41.
19. *Letters*, 685.
20. E. O'Casey, *Seán*, 161.
21. *Ibid.*, 163.
22. *Letters*, 775.
23. *Encyclopedia of the Theatre*, New York 1940, 120–1.
24. Krause, *Seán O'Casey: The Man and his Work*, 161.
25. E. O'Casey, *Seán*, 164–5.
26. *Sunset and Evening Star*, 164.
27. *Ibid.*, 159–60.
28. *Letters*, 617–18.
29. *Ibid.*, 844–5.
30. *Picture Post*, 11 Nov. 1939, quoted in *Letters*, 817–18.
31. *Irish Freedom* (Jan. 1941), quoted in *Letters*, 873–4.
32. Note on the dust-jacket of the 1940 edition of the play, almost certainly written by the playwright.
33. Quoted in R. Ayling and M. J. Durkan, *Seán O'Casey: A Bibliography*, 55–6.
34. *Letters*, 882.
35. A. Simpson, 'O'Casey and the East Wall Area in Dublin', *Irish University Review* X, No. 1 (1980) (Special Issue: *Seán O'Casey: Roots and Branches*).
36. *Pictures in the Hallway*, 335–40.
37. For a full account see Fallon, 152–8.
38. Ayling and Durkan, 76.

39. *Ibid.*, 76.

40. E. O'Casey, *Seán*, 198.
41. *Sunset and Evening Star*, 297–8.
42. *Inishfallen Fare Thee Well*, 13.

Chapter 7: Sunset and Evening Star (pp. 116–136)

1. E. O'Casey, *Seán*, 189.
2. *Sunday Times*, 7 Feb. 1949, quoted in Krause, *Seán O'Casey and his World*, 81.
3. E. O'Casey, *Seán*, 300.
4. Ayling and Durkan, 83.
5. 'O'Casey's Credo', *New York Times*, 9 Nov. 1958.
6. *Encore* (Easter 1956).
7. 'The Bald Primaqueera', *Atlantic Monthly* (Sep. 1965); repr. in *Blasts and Benedictions*, ed. R. Ayling, 63–76.
8. *Ibid.*, 76.
9. Introduction to *Selected Plays of Seán O'Casey*, New York 1954.
10. 'The Hill of Healing' in *I Knock at the Door*, 29–36.
11. E. O'Casey, *Seán*, 233.
12. *The Times*, 1 Mar. 1955.
13. *The Standard* (Dublin), 25 Feb. 1955.
14. *The Green Crow*, 137–8.
15. Krause, *Seán O'Casey: The Man and his Work*, 277.
16. E. O'Casey, *Seán*, 210.
17. 'Under a Greenwood Tree He Died' in *Under a Colored Cap*.
18. Ayling and Durkan, 119–20.
19. *Ibid.*, 123.
20. E. O'Casey, *Eileen*, 189–90.
21. *Letters*, ix.
22. E. O'Casey, *Seán*, 294.

Select Bibliography

Plays

Collected Plays, 4 vols, London 1949–51

Vol. I (1949): *Juno and the Paycock*; *The Shadow of a Gunman*; *The Plough and the Stars*; *The End of the Beginning*; *A Pound on Demand*

Vol. II (1949): *The Silver Tassie*; *Within the Gates*; *The Star Turns Red*

Vol. III (1951): *Purple Dust*; *Red Roses For Me*; *Hall of Healing*

Vol. IV (1951: *Oak Leaves and Lavender*; *Cock-a-Doodle Dandy*; *Bedtime Story*; *Time To Go*

The Bishop's Bonfire, London 1955

The Drums of Father Ned, London 1960

Behind the Green Curtains; *Figuro in the Night*; *The Moon Shines on Kylenamoe: Three Plays by Seán O'Casey*, London 1961

Autobiographical

I Knock at the Door, London 1939

Pictures in the Hallway, London 1942

Drums Under the Window, London 1945

Inishfallen Fare Thee Well, London 1949

Rose and Crown, London 1952

Sunset and Evening Star, London 1955

Mirror in My House, New York 1956 (collected two-volume edition of the above six volumes)

Collections and Other Works

The Story of Thomas Ashe, Dublin 1918

Songs of the Wren, Dublin 1918

More Songs of the Wren, Dublin 1918

The Story of the Irish Citizen Army, Dublin 1919

Windfalls: Stories, Poems and Plays, London 1934

The Flying Wasp, London 1937

The Green Crow, London/New York 1956
Feathers from the Green Crow: Sean O'Casey, 1905–1925, ed. Robert Hogan, London/Columbia, Mo. 1963
Under a Colored Cap: Articles Merry and Mournful with Comments and a Song, London 1963
Blasts and Benedictions: Articles and Stories, selected and ed. by Ronald Ayling, London 1967

Letters

The Letters of Seán O'Casey, Vol. I: *1910–1941*, ed. David Krause, London 1975 (Vols II and III in preparation)

Criticism, Biography, Bibliography

Armstrong, William A., *Seán O'Casey* (Writers and their Work, No. 198), London 1967
Ayling, Ronald, ed., *Seán O'Casey* (Modern Judgments), London 1969; Nashville, Tenn. 1970
Ayling, Ronald, and Durkan, Michael J., *Seán O'Casey: A Bibliography*, London 1978
Benstock, Bernard, *Paycocks and Others: Seán O'Casey's World*, Dublin 1976
Benstock, Bernard, *Seán O'Casey* (Irish Writers Series, ed. James F. Carens), Lewisburg, Pa. 1970
Cowasjee, Saros, *Seán O'Casey: The Man Behind the Plays*, Edinburgh 1963
Fallon, Gabriel, *Seán O'Casey: The Man I Knew*, London 1965
Goldstone, Herbert, *In Search of Community: The Achievement of Seán O'Casey*, Cork 1972
Greaves, C. Desmond, *Seán O'Casey: Politics and Art*, London 1979
Lady Gregory's Journals, 1916–1930, ed. Lennox Robinson, Dublin, 1946
Hogan, Robert, *The Experiments of Seán O'Casey*, New York 1960
Holloway, Joseph, *Impressions of a Dublin Playgoer*, ed. Robert Hogan and Martin J. O'Neill, Illinois 1967
Kilroy, Thomas, ed., *Seán O'Casey: A Collection of Critical Essays*, Englewood Cliffs, NJ 1975
Koslow, J., *The Green and the Red: Seán O'Casey, the Man and his Plays*, New York 1950; rev. ed.: *Seán O'Casey: The Man and his Plays*, New York 1966
Krause, David, *Seán O'Casey: The Man and his Work*, London 1960

Krause, David, *Seán O'Casey and his World*, London 1976
Lowery, Robert G., ed., *The Seán O'Casey Review* (half-yearly review), New York 1975–
McCann, Seán, ed., *The World of Seán O'Casey*, London 1966
Malone, Maureen, *The Plays of Seán O'Casey*, Carbondale, Ill. 1969
Margulies, Martin B., *The Early Life of Seán O'Casey*, Dublin 1970
Mikhail, E. H., *Seán O'Casey: A Bibliography of Criticism*, London 1972
Mikhail, E. H., and O'Riordan, John, ed., *The Sting and the Twinkle: Conversations with Seán O'Casey*, London 1974
O'Casey, Eileen, *Seán*, London 1971
O'Casey, Eileen, *Eileen*, London 1976

Index